RELATIONSHIP ACUITY®

Leadership Through a *Different* Lens

Judy Hemmingsen

Relationship Acuity® is a Registered Trademark in Canada and the United States of America.

Relationship Acuity Copyright © 2021 by RA Leadership Solutions Inc.

All rights reserved. No part of this publication may be reproduced, distributed or transmitted in any form or by any means, including photocopying, recording, or other electronic or mechanical methods, without the prior written permission of the publisher, RA Leadership Solutions Inc. info@ralsolutions.ca, except in the case of brief quotations embodied in critical reviews and certain other non-commercial uses permitted by copyright law.

Relationship Acuity® / Judy Hemmingsen -- 1st ed.

ISBN: 978-1-988925-74-5

TABLE OF CONTENTS

Acknowledgements 1
Preface 3
Introduction: Looking at Leadership Through a Different Lens 5

PART ONE: RELATIONSHIP ACUITY INSIGHTS **11**
   Relationships Matter 15
   The Why Factor 21
   The Perception Connection 39

PART TWO: RELATIONSHIP ACUITY COMPETENCIES **51**
   The Twelve Building Blocks of Leadership 56
   Personal Leadership Competencies 63
      COMPETENCY #1: Acquire Insight Into Self and Others 66
      COMPETENCY #2: Balance Intrinsic Strengths 74
      COMPETENCY #3: Communicate With Influence 87
      COMPETENCY #4 Prevent, Manage, and Resolve Conflict 95
      COMPETENCY #5: Build Resilience 111
   Team Leadership Competencies 127
      COMPETENCY #6: Facilitate Performance Potential 132
      COMPETENCY #7: Coach For Acuity 146
      COMPETENCY #8: Build Cohesive Teams 155
      COMPETENCY #9: Mediate Conflicts 168
      COMPETENCY #10: Lead The People Side of Change 181
   Organizational Leadership Competencies 195
      COMPETENCY #11: Inspire Purpose, Vision, and Values 202
      COMPETENCY #12: Transform Culture 215
   Next Steps: Practice 227
   A Few Final Words 231
   Inspiring Psychologists, Authors, and Educators 233
   Bibliography 235
   About The Author 239

ACKNOWLEDGEMENTS

Many people contributed to the completion of this book. Without their support and belief in me, this book would not have been possible.

A special debt of gratitude goes to my husband and business partner Matt, whose invaluable support and counsel contributed significantly to my finished manuscript. I also owe a great deal of thanks to my associate and good friend Madalena Coutinho, for imparting her illuminating thoughts and perspectives throughout my creative process. Thank you Matt and Maddie!

Many thanks also to my editor, Jess Shulman, who provided her much needed wisdom and professional advice. Jess, you very skillfully took my initial writing to the next level. I couldn't have done it without you.

The vision of my book came to life thanks to the creative team at Prominence Publishing. Thank you Suzanne Doyle-Ingram and Beth Nightingale, for your contributions to the final book design, the cover image, and the publishing process. Your advice has been essential for transforming my manuscript into a polished book.

On a personal level, I would like to acknowledge those who read my manuscript prior to its publication. To Jill Ash, Ron Jockheck and Sarah Matheson – thank you for giving me your valuable time and much appreciated feedback.

Finally, many clients over the course of my career provided me with endless insights and continuous learning that formed the basis of this book. A big thank you to Dr. AB Warriner and the many others who convinced me that I had something worthwhile to say.

PREFACE

After many years consulting with diverse organizations and leaders, I have come to realize that much of my work, initially focused on fixing "people problems," was actually related to the same root cause – people seeing things differently. And seeing is a form of believing. I have coached derailed executives, worked with troubled teams, provided career counselling to disengaged employees, and mediated conflicts. All these interrelated consulting and coaching activities link to differing perceptions, faulty assumptions, and unproductive work relationships.

I clearly remember my very first professional job. I was asked to produce a position paper on the "assessment of management potential." After completing my research and writing, I waited patiently for feedback. Weeks passed, and I heard nothing about it, so I was curious to find out why. I asked my manager, "Who read it? What are the next steps? How will it be applied?" He said something like, "Don't worry, your report is with the powers that be." That was the end of it.

That response took the wind right out of my sails. It seemed to me that my work had had no meaningful outcome. In my view, the task had been purposeless.

But I now realize that other people in my position might not have perceived that situation in the same way. They might have been satisfied just knowing that they had done excellent work that met their own standard. How the work was to be applied might not have mattered so much to them. Someone else might have been frustrated rather than disheartened. They might have expected to see a tangible outcome and, when that was missing, viewed the whole exercise as a waste of their time and effort. Different people can have the same experience and see it from totally different perspectives. On reflection, that experience was a notable leadership lesson for me. The lesson, simply put, is that people differ. They differ in the value they place on the work they do. They also differ in their perception of each situation they encounter.

These differences also include expectations. We differ in the expectations we have of our colleagues and our leaders, and they differ in the expectations they have of us. These differences are rarely expressed or discussed. I expected to be told how my work made a difference, how it met a higher purpose. Why did I assume that my boss knew what I expected? How would anyone know my needs, my expectations, and my

Relationship Acuity: Leadership Through a *Different* Lens

perceptions, particularly since I'd never expressed them? Should the people I worked with intuitively have known how to keep me engaged and committed? Why didn't I speak up? Why wasn't I asked?

Since that time, I have encountered numerous situations that drew attention to differences in perceptions and expectations. On one occasion, I was asked to help a medical research organization transform its managers into, in their words, "nicer people." This organization had a history of promoting its best scientists into people leadership positions. Part of the leadership role was to coach employees, and employees expected coaching support. Unfortunately, the scientists had no desire to coach their employees. What they valued was their research work, and they were rewarded for it. They were not rewarded for the number of hours they spent coaching. So, it was not surprising that they saw no benefit in doing it. While their employees expected guidance and mentoring, the managers expected their employees to leave them alone.

These experiences inspired me to write this book.

Think how often you see people doing things that they see as right, and you see as wrong. You probably react by judging them. You might call them insensitive, unprincipled, careless – just insert any negative trait that you believe applies. What you aren't doing in these cases is stepping back to look for their *why*. Why do people choose to do things you see as wrong or not do things you see as right? Getting to the *why* changes the perceptions you have of them. When you uncover the positive intent behind the behaviour you see, even if you still don't agree with it, you'll understand it. You'll get where people are coming from – you'll see their perspective.

Like most of us, I have difficulty working with people who don't seem to see the world the way I do. It requires hard work to be constantly mindful – to remind myself to seek the reasons people do what they do and try to understand their perspective. That understanding is a gift. With understanding comes respect. And, in today's world, what seems to be missing at all levels of leadership, across government and business and politics, around the globe, is the ability to value different perspectives and to create environments that inspire mutual respect.

I hope this book opens your eyes to new ways of looking at the people and situations you encounter every day. Get to the *why*. Sharpen your perception. Keep your work relationships productive. And see the difference it makes!

INTRODUCTION: LOOKING AT LEADERSHIP THROUGH A DIFFERENT LENS

"The more we lack leadership, the more we hunger for it."
—Warren Bennis

Leadership is as much a pressing challenge today as it was thirty years ago when noted leadership expert Warren Bennis wrote the book *Why Leaders Can't Lead*. Widely regarded as the pioneer of leadership studies, Bennis authored over twenty-five books, and his insights into leadership are still relevant today.

Over the past several decades, leadership has been the subject of much discussion, writing, teaching, and learning. Every organization remains focused on the hiring and development of effective leaders. The challenges Bennis wrote about related to a world that was becoming increasingly complex and diverse. These same challenges exist today, to an even greater extent. Leaders must ride these waves of change while inspiring people, remaining open to new insights and perspectives, and earning trust through influence, not power.

There are as many books on leadership as there are definitions of effective leadership. It's one thing to write about what makes theoretical sense, but quite another to get people to change. Leaders still need coaches. Teams still struggle to operate at peak performance. Organizations still have issues of employee engagement and retention of their best people. Conflict is still present and concealed under boardroom tables. And career-transition coaches continue to guide derailed leaders toward new jobs where they continue to do the same things.

What Is Relationship Acuity® and Why Is It Important?

The guidance and wisdom in this book are inspired by many authors and psychologists. Relationship Acuity is rooted in the psychological theories of relationship management, motivation, perception, and the research of numerous leadership authors that focus on the importance of social and emotional intelligence at work.

Relationship Acuity is best defined as the clarity of perception in one's work relationships. We all know the word *relationship*. It refers to

Relationship Acuity: Leadership Through a *Different* Lens

an association between individuals where each person has the potential to influence the thoughts, feelings, and actions of the other. *Acuity*, on the other hand, is not a word we often see in leadership writings. Yet, acuity is particularly important in the field of leadership development. In the context of this book, it refers to the sharpness in one's perception of the situations and people around them. Together, the words relationship and acuity form a critical leadership skill. You can regard it as the lens of leadership in work relationships.

Relationship Acuity and the Three Levels of Leadership

You might equate leadership with management. But leadership is more than that. It has nothing to do with a job title or a position of power. I define a leader as someone others choose to follow. To get people to follow you, you need to build healthy relationships and mutual understanding. When you understand the people you work with, and they understand you, you build trust and mutual respect. In this leadership context, having Relationship Acuity means that you have honed the personal and interpersonal competencies you need in order to work productively with others.

The Relationship Acuity model is illustrated on the following page. There are three levels of leadership, each requiring a specific set of personal and interpersonal competencies. These competencies build on each other and also complement one another, working together to form the broad spectrum of leadership capabilities that exemplify Relationship Acuity.

Introduction: Looking at Leadership Through a *Different* Lens

THE RELATIONSHIP ACUITY LEADERSHIP MODEL

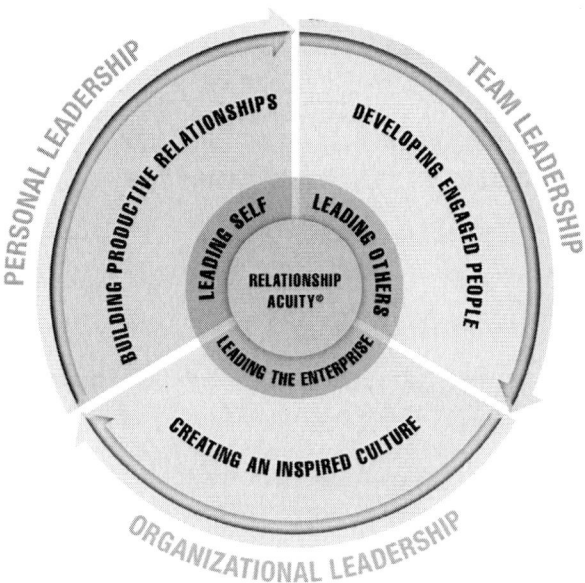

Leadership begins at the personal level, right at the start of your career. It starts with your ability to build productive relationships with the people you rely on to get your work done. You have to lead yourself before you can lead others. Personal leadership means entering every interaction with mindfulness of the situation and the people involved. You will often be challenged to work with many people with different and distinct ways of looking at things. Every day, your colleagues are watching your behaviour, listening to the words you choose, and judging you based on their personal perceptions. In this regard, you must constantly think about how you act and interact with others. Although it's easy to ignore the importance of your work relationships when you're focused on results, ironically, the more productive your relationships, the stronger your results will be.

Once you start leading teams, your role requires additional competencies that enable you to engage your employees to do their best and achieve their potential. As a team leader, you can help your team members build Relationship Acuity by sharing your insights from this book.

If and when you reach the executive level of an organization, your role then is to create an enterprise-wide culture that inspires people to follow your vision and purpose, and live the values of your organization.

Relationship Acuity: Leadership Through a *Different* Lens

About This Book

This book is the result of many years of leadership consulting, coaching, and facilitation. Over the years, I have been lucky to gather many fascinating insights about the working world. Here are my top ten:

1. No one works in isolation. Whether you're an individual contributor, a team leader, or an executive, the only way to get your job done is to work productively with others.

2. Most people don't realize the critical role that perception plays in attempting to influence others.

3. Many organizations talk about leadership development before they even begin to define what being a leader means.

4. Employee engagement and discretionary effort are driven by each person's intrinsic motivation, not by company bonuses and salary increases.

5. Leaders need to follow the Platinum Rule, not the Golden Rule. The Golden Rule says that people should treat others as they, themselves, want to be treated. The Platinum Rule understands that people differ in what they value and expect from others, and that one size doesn't fit all.

6. A person's job performance is most often assessed on the achievement of set goals and objectives – *what* they are required to do. Rarely does it focus on their behaviours – *how* they're expected to do it.

7. When people lose jobs, it's rarely because of a lack of competence or ability. Instead, it's usually because they have failed to work well with others.

8. The widely accepted Peter Principle, put forward by educator Lawrence J. Peter in the 1970s, states that each person tends to rise to their level of incompetence. In reality, this principle has more to do with passion than capability: People don't become incompetent; they just become indifferent.

9. During change, leaders struggle with finding ways to inspire commitment and engagement, so they rarely do so.

10. Executives usually agree on mutually defined organizational values yet differ in how they demonstrate those values each day.

These insights inspired this book. Each one points to the important role that relationships, motivation, and perception play in today's complex, ever-changing work environments. We've all learned valuable concepts from a myriad of wise leadership authors. Yet nothing has really changed.

Despite this, I remain hopeful that positive change starts with inspiring just one person. It's like the old saying about how to eat an elephant... one bite at a time. Each person who is inspired becomes an agent of change. That's the purpose of this book. Perhaps after reading this book, you will, in turn, influence those who work with you. The change agent could be you.

Will You Benefit from Reading This Book?

If you agree that leadership is about working with people, not just about accomplishing goals and getting things done, then this book is for you. You will learn how to influence and inspire the people you need to help you achieve your success.

This book addresses many leadership challenges, and it's intended to change your perspective about them. It will take you from insight through to actionable ideas. Whether you need to influence or engage others, gain their commitment, or communicate in more impactful ways, this book will help.

You will be introduced to twelve leadership competencies. These competencies represent the personal and interpersonal skills embedded in the three levels of leadership. Great leaders demonstrate these competencies that enable them to lead self, lead others, and lead the organization. These skills can be learned, practiced, and honed. It doesn't matter whether you're a member of a team, the leader of a team, or the leader of an organization – think of these competencies as your building blocks for success.

Relationship Acuity: Leadership Through a *Different* Lens

The Relationship Acuity Leadership Guidebook – From Reflection to Practice

This book is chock full of valuable insights, new perspectives, and actionable ideas. However, insight alone doesn't lead to new practices. You may remember those times when things didn't turn out as expected – maybe you couldn't get others to agree with you, or you lost a sale to a critical customer; maybe someone just didn't get your point of view, or you just couldn't get someone to do what you needed them to do, no matter how hard you tried. Each of these situations could have ended differently with a different approach. Change your approach and you're bound to get better results the next time around. The *Relationship Acuity Leadership Guidebook* was developed for this purpose. It takes the insights from this book to the next level by providing specific, practical applications and follow-up activities for each of the twelve Relationship Acuity competencies. So, think of *this* book as your introductory training program – Relationship Acuity 101. Then, the follow-up *Guidebook* is your how-to guide for specific on-the-job applications. For maximum benefit, you'll want to read both.

How to Read This Book

To learn **WHY** the concepts of Relationship Acuity are important to leadership development, read Part One.

To learn **WHAT** leadership competencies are required at each of the Personal, Team, and Organizational levels of leadership, read Part Two.

To learn **HOW** to apply the concepts in this book, work through the competency practices in the *Relationship Acuity Leadership Guidebook*.

PART ONE: RELATIONSHIP ACUITY INSIGHTS

The Foundation: Motivation, Perception, And Behaviour

Relationship Acuity focuses on the important role that motivation, perception, and behaviour each play in our work relationships.

The figure below shows how these flow together, starting on the left with your motivation. I call this motivation your *Intrinsic Driver*. *Intrinsic* means innate and essential to each of us, not something that we can change or learn. Your intrinsic driver is your motivation to achieve a sense of self-worth and purpose in your life.

Your intrinsic driver frames the perceptions you have of yourself and others. This is what makes you see something one way, while others might see it differently.

Your perceptions, in turn, drive your behaviour.

The behaviours that align with our intrinsic driver are called our *intrinsic strengths*. We know we're using these strengths when we feel good about what we're doing or saying – it feels right to us. That's why people differ in the ways they behave, because their behaviour is driven by their personal intrinsic driver and perceptions.

Here's the premise of Relationship Acuity: While we can't change our motivation, we do have the ability to change our perceptions and, ultimately, how we act and interact with others. That's the secret sauce of great leadership!

THE FLOW
THE LINK BETWEEN MOTIVATION, PERCEPTION AND BEHAVIOUR

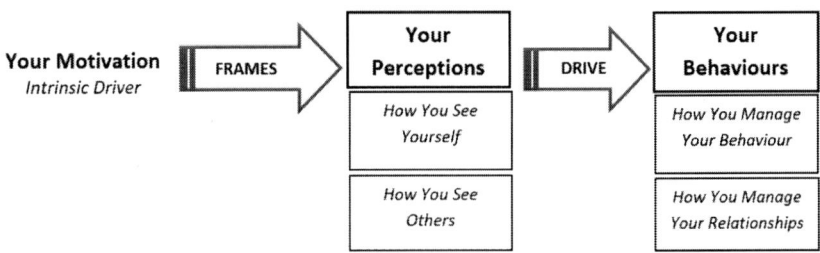

Perceptions play a powerful role in leadership, influencing every work relationship we have. Differences between how two people view the world are not always visible. That's why people very often misinterpret other people's intentions. You can probably think of many times

Part One: Relationship Acuity Insights

you have made an assumption about someone, only to find out later that you'd misread their intent. Many conflicts are rooted in these misperceptions. When you see the behaviour, you assume the intent.

Many theories of motivation focus solely on universal human motives, but I believe we need to go deeper – to the reason people behave as they do. Relationship Acuity is founded on the belief that every interaction you have is influenced by your intrinsic driver and how it frames your perception at that time. Like most people, you're probably not even aware that this driver exists, let alone the role it plays in determining how you look at situations. But it's there, influencing how you see things and guiding how you interact with others. And it's the quality of those interactions that ultimately determine your success. Developing acuity means learning to shift your perceptions – in other words, to change your perspective and your behaviour. We'll delve further into these concepts in the chapters ahead.

RELATIONSHIPS MATTER

> *"Nothing lives alone... reality is created through*
> *our participation in relationships. We choose what*
> *to notice; we relate to certain things and ignore*
> *others. Through these chosen relationships,*
> *we create our world."*
> —Margaret Wheatley

I think it's safe to say that, when it comes to leadership, relationships matter. Jim Kouzes and Barry Posner, authors of the best-selling book *The Leadership Challenge*, stress that success in leadership is a function of human relationships – how well people work together. Every day, you interact with co-workers, colleagues, customers, clients, and bosses. Each relationship is important when it comes to getting your work done. You can't just walk away from a person that irritates you. You can't say, "it doesn't matter that I don't have a good relationship with them," because it matters a lot!

Like most of us, you are probably in work relationships with a few people who you'd rather not work with at all, given the choice. You probably see these relationships as, at the very least, challenging. What if you were to look at those relationships in a different way? What if you could see them as opportunities for new insights? You might learn something that could make a difference when it comes to your work performance. One of my executive clients, Ken, found himself in a career crisis when he failed to pay attention to his important work relationships. Throughout his career, Ken focused on the goals and objectives he needed to achieve. His technical skills got him up the ladder. He was even tagged to be the next CEO of his company. Then, his career derailed. He hadn't paid much attention to the people he needed support from on the way up. As a result, his colleagues didn't respect him. They didn't see him as a team player. He was too competitive. He didn't listen to other perspectives. They hadn't forgotten the times he'd "lost his cool" in management meetings. When it came time for his peer performance ratings, Ken's results were dismal. Getting this feedback from his colleagues was a life-changing event. He had put everything he'd worked for at risk. In his own words, he was "humbled." Managing his relationships became his most important leadership challenge.

We know that leadership is as much based on the people as on the work that needs to get done. That's because no one works by themselves or achieves results without the help or input of others. So, to be an effective leader, you need to own your relationships. That means looking at leadership through a different lens. When you do that, you begin to gain some insight into the people you work with and for. How often do you reflect on the quality of your work relationships? Are they healthy and productive? Do you value the people you work with? Do they value you? Do you have any insights regarding their strengths, their ways of working, and what they care about? It seems logical to pay attention to these insights, but most of us are too busy to take the time to do so.

The people you work with are both like you and different from you. Just like you, each has their own internal motivation. Each person may want to do things differently and for different reasons. And each has a preferred way of getting things done that is not necessarily your way. Each person's behaviour is linked to what *they* value most. You may tend to look at these different behaviours and judge people according to what you see. That's focusing on *what* they do. First, you need to learn *why* they do it. That's an important insight.

What Does It Mean to Be a Leader?

New leadership books are published all the time. They all promise a fresh perspective. But if you look closely, most books offer different ways of looking at similar concepts. As yet, no one has found *the one* definitive explanation of what leadership means in practical terms. That's because it's a complex concept. You probably have your own thoughts about leadership, based on what you believe an ideal leader looks like to you.

I look at leadership as a jigsaw puzzle with lots of pieces. The question is, which pieces are most important? That's hard to answer because each person has a different opinion. It depends on who you're asking. No small wonder people become confused when management tells them to "hone their leadership skills." They wonder, "what does that mean? Is it my personal attributes, my attitude, my expected behaviours, my skills, my qualities? What skills? What behaviours? What

Relationships Matter

qualities?" The answers will differ, depending on the person you are asking. Each person has their own unique perspective.

The many pieces in this puzzle, when fitted together, provide a more complete picture. Each piece is important. In many leadership theories, the concept of *relationships* is often overlooked. Sometimes it's implied. A study by the Carnegie Foundation and Stanford University conducted many years ago concluded that 85% of job success comes from having well-developed "people" skills. So, what does it mean to have people skills? Generally, it means having the ability to influence and communicate effectively with other people and to relate in ways that are mutually productive.

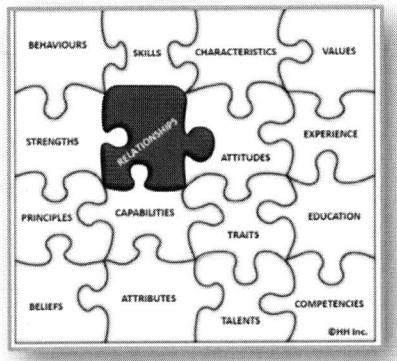

When I say that leadership requires engaging in productive relationships, that probably sounds a little too simple. It's true that *relationships* are not the only piece in the leadership puzzle. But it's undoubtedly one of the most important ones.

This Is Where Perception Fits In

We rarely see much written about the importance of perception in leadership and, more importantly, how it influences the way people relate to each other. Yet, perception is critical in leadership. It has an impact on everything you do. It influences how you look at situations and the people you encounter every day. It unconsciously controls everything you do and say. As a result, your perceptions can positively or negatively affect those work relationships that matter most to you.

I once had a coaching client named Elaine, whose boss believed she needed to develop better leadership skills. In a meeting, I asked her boss what he meant by better leadership skills. He replied, "Well, she's got to act faster on things. There's a major problem in her department, and she's done nothing about it." As he talked about this issue, he was describing in detail what he believed a leader needed to do when faced with an issue to resolve. He wanted to see her deal swiftly with the matter in an authoritative way. To him, she appeared to be avoiding the problem.

But when I spoke with Elaine, she made her perception clear: she believed in the importance of taking time to think about her response. She wasn't avoiding; she was problem-solving. She didn't think she lacked the required skills or knowledge; she simply believed that acting too swiftly could cause even further issues. That sounded reasonable.

Elaine's behaviour did not reflect what her boss expected her to do, so some coaching may have been necessary. But before taking that step, I clearly saw that I needed to address the relationship between Elaine and her boss. This relationship was unproductive because he never communicated his expectations, and neither of them mentioned what they saw as the required or desired response. Elaine and her boss demonstrated that each had their own perspective on the meaning of leadership. To one, it meant a swift response. To another, it meant risk mitigation and careful due diligence. No one person's perspective is ever the right one (although we're all sure the right one is our own!). Sometimes the best solutions come from sharpening our own focus, understanding a different perspective, and reaching a mutual agreement.

Perceiving Root Causes, Not Symptoms

Elaine's story reminds us that what seems like a specific problem is actually only a symptom of a relationship management issue. You probably have seen many without recognizing them as such. However, they are quite obvious when you see open confrontation, hostility, human rights complaints, declining productivity or performance, poor morale, turnover, health/ stress leave, union/management and boss/subordinate disputes, active resistance to change... the list can go on and on! If these are the symptoms of relationship issues, there should be a solution that goes beyond the symptoms to the root causes. A solution often gets rid of the symptoms, but it's never a cure. Dig deeper for the root causes. You can bet that if they're ignored, the symptoms will return time and time again.

A municipal government client of mine was concerned about how their managers were handling the performance of their employees. There were too many employee disputes. They wanted to hold a performance management workshop to teach their managers how to have constructive conversations with their direct reports. The course, however, wasn't the right solution at all. Although we did run the course and the managers did learn some valuable skills and techniques, they all said that they expected to have had a hard time applying them. An open, honest, and constructive dialogue was virtually impossible to have with their employees, they said, because a union steward always had to be in the room at the same time. The root cause of the problem wasn't a lack of supervisory knowledge or skill. It was the organization's adversarial union/management relationship that needed to be addressed.

In a similar situation, I worked with a financial services firm that was going through a major change initiative. Everyone was stressed. Morale was low. They decided to develop a training program to help people manage their stress. Stress, however, was the symptom, not the root cause. The managers needed to understand how to support their employees during a period of rapid change. This was a change-management issue. The employees were stressed because they didn't trust their leaders and they feared losing their jobs.

Let's look at the faulty treatment of symptoms through the lens of the medical profession. We have all experienced a headache at one time or another – that's a symptom. The solution is usually to take a painkiller. That gets rid of the headache, but the symptom returns. So, you take another pill... and the cycle of treating the symptom continues, at least until you realize the headache won't stop coming back. Then, finally, you wonder if maybe there's something causing that headache that needs to be addressed. What might be the potential root cause of a headache? It could be stress, lack of sleep, overindulgence in alcohol, lack of food, eye strain, or even a more serious medical issue. There's no way of knowing until you look deeper at each situation and circumstance.

Many issues in organizations are the symptoms of unhealthy relationships. Yet, we rarely see *relationship management* training as the first response. Training programs continue to address symptoms, not root causes. When faulty relationships are the root cause, address that issue first.

Faulty relationships often stem from people seeing the world in different ways. A conflict is almost always rooted in people having strong opinions based on different perspectives. To consider why that happens, think back on the flow from the previous chapter. Everything we do flows from our inner driver to our outward behaviour. You can't see

Part One: Relationship Acuity Insights

a person's inner motivation – it's their invisible *why*. You can only see what they're doing or hear what they say. When someone makes the comment "this is how I see it," they're looking at things from their own particular perspective. That perspective might be different from yours. It's best not to make assumptions or judge someone before you find out why they see things the way they do. Seeking insight into why people do what they do helps build trust and mutual respect. Understanding someone is not the same as liking them. With understanding, comes the wisdom of knowing someone well enough to keep the work relationship healthy and productive.

THE WHY FACTOR

"Millions saw the apple fall, but Newton was the one who asked why." — Bernard Baruch

A motive is a reason for doing something. Work environments most often refer to *extrinsic* motivation. Extrinsic motivators are external to a person. They include things like benefits, bonuses, salaries, titles, perks, and promotions. These are rewards offered to ensure that people conform to the expectations of others. This book is not about extrinsic motivation.

The focus of Relationship Acuity is *intrinsic* motivation. Intrinsic implies something within you that is unique to you – it's your *why*. It frames how you see the world around you and forms your assumptions and judgments about yourself and others. These assumptions and judgments determine how you act and interact with the people around you. Your motivation is your intrinsic driver. As we saw earlier, it's at the root of your perceptions and your behaviours.

When you gain a deeper understanding of your intrinsic driver, you become more mindful of the things you personally care about. This mindfulness also enables you to understand what drives others – what they care about. With this insight, you are taking the first step toward preventing conflict and preserving productive work relationships.

Our Drive for Self-Worth

Most of us aren't aware of our intrinsic driver, nor its link to our need for self-worth. But it's there. It's our constant energizer that drives us to do those things that provide us with a sense of purpose and satisfaction. We are all inspired to achieve goals that matter most to us. Think about the times you've been challenged to achieve things that you believe are important and have a purpose. When you achieve those things, you have activated your own internal generator. You feel endless energy to keep going.

Now, think about the times when you had to do something because someone else expected you to do it, but it wasn't inspiring. You probably had to look for ways to maintain your energy and keep going.

Part One: Relationship Acuity Insights

The ability to recognize what drives another person plays a major role in keeping relationships productive. Recognizing each person's sense of purpose and understanding that people differ in what they deem important is a huge step toward improving relationships.

Let me illustrate this point with a story. A visitor to Europe was passing by a cathedral undergoing reconstruction. He noticed two workers performing similar tasks. One worker looked cheerful and engaged. He whistled as he placed bricks into his wheelbarrow and transported them across the yard. The second worker looked tired and grumpy. The visitor asked this seemingly unhappy worker what he was doing. "Just what it looks like!" he answered with a scowl. "I'm loading bricks and hauling them across the yard." When the more cheerful worker returned, the visitor asked him the same question. That worker replied, "I'm helping to rebuild our cathedral."

This tale highlights the importance of finding purpose in our work. When we have a sense of purpose, in even the most menial tasks, we can find all kinds of energy and drive to get them done. It wasn't the task of moving bricks that engaged this worker; it was the end goal.

People who are fulfilling their sense of purpose in their work are more engaged, more committed, and more willing to increase their discretionary effort. You may not have thought about it much, but you can probably think of times at work when you have been truly inspired and felt you were contributing to something larger than yourself. Maybe you went above and beyond what was required, pouring extra effort into your work and reaching higher levels of performance.

Aaron Hurst, author of *The Purpose Economy*, asserts that everyone wants and needs to find purpose in their work. According to Hurst, money often conflicts with finding purpose. It is a poor substitute for a definition of success. Purpose is a universal motivation. It's a direction, not a destination. One of the most famous advocates for purpose was Viktor Frankl, who wrote about the importance of purpose in the concentration camps during the Holocaust. He found that purpose was the key to his survival. In *Man's Search for Meaning*, he wrote, "Life is never made unbearable by circumstances, but only by lack of meaning and purpose. Evermore people today have the means to live, but no meaning to live for."

Your sense of purpose is your personal mission in life. It inspires you, empowers you, motivates you, and gives meaning to everything you do.

There's a big difference between a reason for doing something and the purpose for doing it. If you were to ask yourself why you work, your answer might be "to make money." Making money is your reason for working. Now, to get to your purpose, you must go deeper to the aspect of your work that feeds your self-worth. When someone says they go to work "to make a difference," to "improve a process," or to "achieve a goal," those answers are more reflective and more definitive of that person's sense of purpose. They go beyond the need to earn money. Each person's sense of purpose reflects what they personally value most. So, from a leadership perspective, you can see why it's important to recognize that what you value may only be valued by *some* others, not *all* others.

Discovering your purpose starts with reflecting on the moments when you felt most engaged in your work. These are the times when your efforts helped you to feel energized rather than drained. What were you doing at the time? Review your thoughts and then look for patterns.

Many years ago, when I worked in a consulting organization, I was offered a promotion that required a choice between my professional purpose and a potential management position. The role offered a higher salary and status than my current role did. However, it was a role that I genuinely didn't want. My purpose is rooted in the need to make a difference – to help clients through coaching and group facilitation. If I'd accepted the management role, I would have had to do more administration and less consulting. Of course, had I accepted this new role I would have made every effort to do the best job, but my heart wouldn't have been in it. After a period of time, I would probably have been asked to leave the firm. There's a price to pay when the job doesn't fit with what you value. The energy required to overcome the constant frustration and stress is just not sustainable. In this case, I was fortunate to have the opportunity to negotiate an alternative solution that fit both my needs and those of the organization. Often, that's not the case. People are usually reticent to speak up or fearful that declining an offer will be a career-limiting move. They think they have no choice. So they accept and, sadly, see their energy and their performance potential drain away.

The rewards you get from your job have much less to do with the actual work you do and everything to do with what you deem important. It's your perception of your work that counts. It may be repetitive, even stressful work, but if you perceive what you do as purposeful, you will generate an endless supply of energy to get it done. Remember the brick layer? He had all kinds of energy to keep moving those bricks! Now, ask yourself, "Is my work just a job? Is it just the paycheque that allows me to enjoy what I do when I'm not at work? Am I a TGIF person?" If you answer yes, it may be time to look at the degree to which your job fulfills your sense of purpose.

In 1943, Abraham Maslow wrote *A Theory of Human Motivation*, which provided what's become a classic depiction of human motivation. From this theory, he developed a five-tier pyramid model of human needs depicting a hierarchical ranking. The two lowest levels of the pyramid constitute our Basic Physiological and Security needs. These needs are of primary importance. In a work context, they equate to the needs for fair pay and benefits, a harm-free workplace, a secure job, and the necessary resources to do the job. These needs motivate us primarily when they are missing. Once they're met, we naturally strive for more.

Progressing up the pyramid, the needs become increasingly related to our growth and development. Think of times when you felt the need to contribute as a member of a team (the need for *belonging*) or to be respected for your contributions (the need for *esteem*).

The top tier is about our *self-actualization* needs – the need to grow to our fullest potential. This need is closely linked to our self-worth and sense of purpose. Each person perceives self-actualization in their own way, based on what they personally value. In an organizational context, the need for self-actualization explains why many people stay engaged in their work even during challenging times: they perceive that their work has meaning.

MASLOW'S HIERARCHY OF NEEDS
(adapted from "A Theory of Human Motivation" A. H. Maslow (1943))

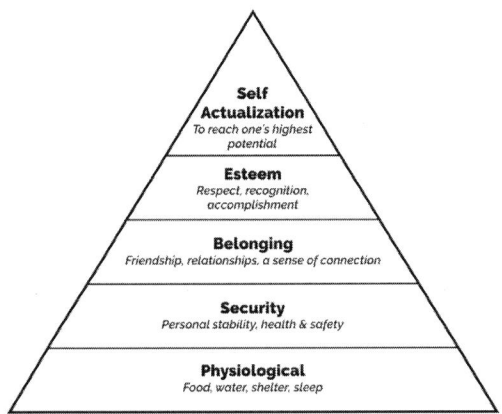

Energy Comes from Purpose

Most people don't recognize their purpose as a source of energy. Our energy is an unlimited resource that is constantly generated when we are doing what we value most – the things that give us a sense of meaning in our life. We spend 40 to 60% of our waking hours at work. Some people thrive during that time, while others just survive. What do you do during that time that gives you energy and initiative? Remember, although time is a limited resource, your energy is renewable, depending upon what you choose to do with that time.

How do you feel at the end of the day? If you're exhausted and drained of all energy, it may be a signal that you perceive your work as offering no meaning. It doesn't fulfill that deeper sense of purpose. So ask yourself, from your perspective, why is your work important?

The amount of energy and commitment you put into your job provides the measure of your discretionary effort. If you perform just at the level that's acceptable and expected, you are expending just enough effort to keep your job. You could probably find more energy, but maybe you can't be bothered to generate it. *Discretionary effort* is the amount of extra effort you put in, above and beyond the "acceptable" level. Ask yourself, how much discretionary effort do you give to your current job?

If you honestly believe you demonstrate a high level of discretionary effort, it's likely that you see your work as more than just a job to get

Part One: Relationship Acuity Insights

done. You care about what you do and how you do it. Your work brings rewards that are meaningful. Your work is integral to your self-worth. This generates commitment. There's an old saying that, at a breakfast of eggs and bacon, the chicken is a willing participant, but the pig is, without doubt, committed. With commitment, you're all in!

Amy Wrzesniewski, a psychologist at the Yale School of Management, researches the way people make meaning of their work. She found that people who consider their work to be a calling or purpose tend to be more satisfied than those who think of their work as "just a job." And having a calling is not restricted to people in white-collar positions. For example, Wrzesniewski interviewed hospital janitors who believed they had a calling. They saw their work as more than cleaning; it was about helping support patient healing. She demonstrates a strong correlation between seeing work as meaningful and overall health and well-being. I have personally worked with many people who are stressed, tired, in conflict, and disengaged at work. Many of them take medical leave. Their mental and physical health suffers because something is missing. By contrast, work that inspires drives people to do more.

Throughout my career, I have coached countless people who have been asked to leave their organizations for a variety of reasons. As people go through a career transition process, I counsel them to look in the rear-view mirror to see their previous role and work environment with fresh eyes. I find that when faced with finding a new job, younger clients tend to focus on finding a similar job in a new organization, whereas people in mid-career begin to shift their focus from getting another job to searching for more fulfilling work. Through reflection, many realize that, up to that point in their career, their work has not been very fulfilling. At some point, they stopped learning, contributing, or deriving any form of satisfaction in the workplace, instead looking for those things in activities outside of work. When faced with the prospect of working for many more years to come, they begin to think about choosing a different path.

My client Karen is a good example of this phenomenon. Karen was a corporate lawyer who had previously worked in several law firms and organizations. Downsizing or reorganizing were always the reasons her former employers chose to let her go. However, Karen was sure that the real reason was that most of the time, she felt she was "running on empty." Her performance was mediocre, not due to a lack of capability, but because the work didn't inspire her. When I asked why she'd chosen law as her career, she pointed to pressure from her father. He was a lawyer and it seemed like a good idea for her to become a lawyer too. At that time, what neither Karen nor her father understood was that legal work was rewarding for him, not her. Constant stress and lack of interest in her work were important signals that she had ignored for many years. Eventually, Karen chose to change her career. She returned to school and became a teacher. Her passion was to help kids learn and grow.

Most of the high-school students Karen taught had difficulty understanding why she chose to teach rather than work in law. They couldn't see why she wouldn't prefer the status, power, and money that the legal profession offered. Karen had a unique perspective to share with her students. Her message was simply that people perform at their best when they have energy and passion for the work they do. When that's lacking, it's time to do something else.

For years, I have heard the same question from managers. How can I get someone to be motivated at work? The answer is quite simple. If a person isn't motivated, it's because they perceive their work, or the results of their work, to be meaningless. Why do more than necessary if it doesn't matter? The worst-case scenario is when neither the task nor the result is intrinsically rewarding. The work gets done, but at what level of performance?

Every person is always influenced by their own internal query: "what's in it for me?" (WIIFM). The answer might be "it's my job and I have to do it" or "if I don't do it, I'll lose my job." If those are your answers, it's not likely that you're getting any intrinsic reward from your work. The only reason you do it is because it's your job.

Ideally, you want to be engaged in tasks that achieve *meaningful* outcomes. Even if the task itself is one that you don't specifically enjoy doing, if the outcome is meaningful and matters to you, you will have the drive to achieve it.

Now, pick one aspect of your job – think first about it as a task that needs to get done. Now think of it as a calling. Do you feel a shift in energy? Pay attention to how this different perspective impacts your sense of purpose.

Is your work draining your energy? Think about the level of effort you are giving to your team and your organization. It might just be the minimum effort required. It might not be the best you can do. Give yourself a quick checkup. If you have five or more check marks on the list below, your work is probably not generating much energy.

- ☐ I see my job as a means to make money
- ☐ I see no purpose in what I do
- ☐ I don't enjoy my work
- ☐ I find that time goes slowly during the day
- ☐ I often think of doing other things
- ☐ I find it hard to focus my attention on the task at hand
- ☐ I feel exhausted at the end of the day
- ☐ I look forward to Fridays
- ☐ I dread Monday mornings
- ☐ I wish I could make a living doing something else

Time for Introspection

It's up to you to keep yourself engaged and productive in your work life. To do these things well, you need to cultivate a deeper understanding of yourself. Clarify what matters to you. When you find the right role, you'll find fulfillment. In our careers, we are often dictated by external demands. Most of us never ask ourselves, "Why is my work important?" Our tasks are often defined by a job description with a list of tasks. So, ask yourself why your job is important. To answer, you need to look at what your current work situation requires. What results are you required to achieve that will make a difference? What is your unique contribution? How can you make the greatest contribution to what needs to be done?

Remember: Purpose Creates Passion

Robert J. Kriegel, in his book *If It Ain't Broke, BREAK IT*, tells a story of interviewing over five hundred top performers from all areas of work. He says, "One quality they had in common was *passion*! It was their drive, their enthusiasm, their desire that distinguished them. They were passionate and excited about what they were doing." Kriegel goes on to describe what a top executive recruiter had to say when asked about the qualities he looked for in a leader. "The thing that makes the difference between a good manager and an inspiring, dynamic leader goes beyond competence. It's *passion.* That is the single quality that is going to lift a person head and shoulders above the rest..."

Passion is no ordinary word. It's the spark that inspires and taps into your energy resources. It's truly connected to your sense of purpose, and it fosters your commitment. Reflect on your level of passion for your work. Rate it from one to ten. If the number is six or lower, consider why that might be.

Education, skills, and experience allow you to be good at what you do. That's acceptable. It's okay to be good. But with passion, you can move from good to exceptional. When you're energized by what you're doing, you feel different. You won't see your work as something you have to do. You'll see it as something you want to do. You'll see it as rewarding. You'll persevere when things get tough.

Think about the impact of your work in the context of Maslow's self-actualization needs. What do you want to be remembered for? When you imagine your retirement party, what do you want people to say? What will have given you a sense of purpose in your life?

Discover Your Sense of Purpose

Let's start by looking at how people differ in what they value. Picture yourself entering a room where people stand in three different circles. They congregate together because they share similar interests. Each group can be thought of as a community of purpose. Each community represents what is most important to the people in that group when they're working toward a goal or faced with a challenge.

Review the three groups below and reflect on which group (or groups) is similar to you and why.

1. **Group One:** This group's purpose is related to results, work productivity, and goal achievement. They believe in the importance of getting things done without delay. They value organizing resources and directing others to achieve goals in a timely way. They care about recognition, tangible rewards, and increased levels of responsibility.

2. **Group Two:** This group's purpose is related to relationships, helping people, and providing service. They believe that the people within an organization contribute to its success. They

care about how people are treated and whether they are valued and getting the support they need. They want work relationships to be positive and conflict to be prevented where possible. They believe that people are most productive in an environment that allows them to grow and deliver their best work.

3. **Group Three:** This group's purpose is related to reason, autonomy, and quality. They believe that the work must be done the right way, through thoughtful due diligence, orderly process, and risk mitigation. They value working independently and being recognized for their experience and expertise. They believe that thoroughness and quality control ensure that the path toward the goal is the correct one to take.

Each group represents a distinct intrinsic driver. These drivers frame our perceptions and ultimately influence how we act and interact with others. They fulfill our need for self-worth and meaning in life. The drivers referenced in this book stem from theories of intrinsic motivation written by four noted psychologists of the last century. Their theories are summarized in the following chart.

FOUR THEORIES OF INTRINSIC MOTIVATION

Psychologist	Theory	Intrinsic Motivation
Edward L. Deci	Self-Determination Theory	**Competence:** *Seeking to control outcomes* **Relatedness:** *Seeking to connect with others* **Autonomy:** *Seeking to be in control of one's life*
David McClelland	Three Needs Theory	**Power:** *Thriving on being in charge* **Affiliation:** *Thriving on working with others* **Achievement:** *Thriving on solving problems*
Karen Horney	Theory of Neurosis	**Expansion:** *The need for power and control over others* **Compliance:** *The need for pleasing others and being liked by them* **Withdrawal:** *The need for self-sufficiency and independence*
Elias H. Porter	Relationship Awareness Theory	**Assertive – Directing:** *Wanting to direct people* **Altruistic – Nurturing:** *Wanting to help people* **Analytic – Autonomizing:** *Wanting to be self-dependent*

The three Relationship Acuity drivers represented in this book are:

1. **The Drive for Achievement –** a primary focus on ***results*** (producing an outcome)

Part One: Relationship Acuity Insights

2. **The Drive for Affiliation** – a primary focus on *relationships* (connecting with others)

3. **The Drive for Autonomy** – a primary focus on *reason* (engaging in logical thought)

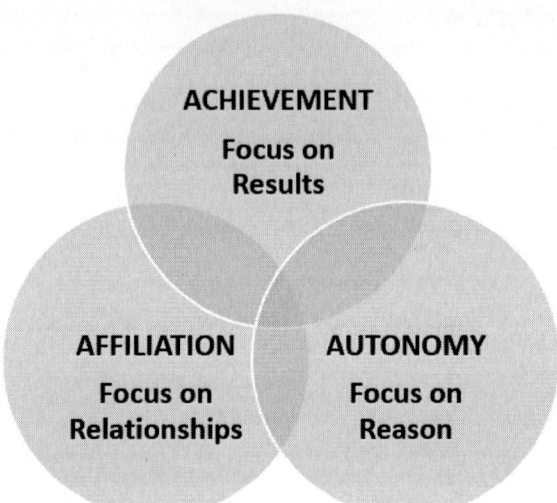

These drivers are often experienced as incompatible and the differences between them can be sources of conflict in the workplace.

To further consider which group is most like you, reflect on the following statements:

The Drive for Achievement

- ☐ I value directing others in getting a task done
- ☐ I focus on the efficiency and effectiveness of my work
- ☐ It is important to overcome a challenge and be viewed as focused and in control
- ☐ Achieving a goal gives me a sense of self-worth

If you placed a check mark in most of the above, achievement may be your primary driver.

The Drive for Affiliation

- ☐ I value giving help to others
- ☐ I focus on the impact of my work on others
- ☐ It is important to provide a service to others and be viewed as loyal and trustworthy
- ☐ Building positive work relationships gives me a sense of self-worth

If you placed a check mark in most of the above, affiliation may be your primary driver.

The Drive for Autonomy

- ☐ I value putting things in order
- ☐ I focus on the logic and accuracy of my work
- ☐ It is important to work autonomously and be viewed as proficient and reliable
- ☐ Relying on my own capabilities gives me a sense of self-worth

If you placed a check mark in most of the above, autonomy may be your primary driver.

What If I Checked Boxes in More Than One Group?

It's entirely possible to have a combination of drivers. You may feel internal conflict and be unaware of its source. Internal conflict occurs when you are equally drawn by two or three drivers that seem opposed to one another.

Here's how overlapping drivers can be experienced:

ACHIEVEMENT + AFFILIATION: Equal Regard for Both Results and Relationships

If these two drivers both resonate, you probably feel the need to get things done and to ensure people are okay. Both are important to you. Too much of either one can result in delaying the result or risk making people upset. Neither would be an ideal outcome. Your challenge is to satisfy both priorities.

Part One: Relationship Acuity Insights

ACHIEVEMENT + AUTONOMY: Equal Regard for Both Results and Reason

If these two drivers both resonate, you probably feel the need to get things done and to ensure they are done correctly. Both are important to you. Too much of either one can result in delaying the result or risking the quality of the work. Neither would be an ideal outcome. Your challenge is to satisfy both priorities.

AFFILIATION + AUTONOMY: Equal Regard for Both Relationships and Reason

If these two drivers both resonate, you probably feel the need to make sure people are okay and to ensure things are done correctly. Both are important to you. Too much of either one can result in you either ignoring the help that is needed or being distracted from the work at hand. Neither would be an ideal outcome. Your challenge is to satisfy both priorities.

ACHIEVEMENT + AFFILIATION + AUTONOMY: Equal Regard for Results, Relationships, and Reason

If all three drivers resonate for you, you probably feel the need to get things done, to make sure people are okay, and to ensure things are done correctly. All three are important to you. Three conflicting priorities can be exhausting. It may be difficult to see one as most important. For you, it's *all* important. Your challenge is to satisfy all three priorities.

Does Your Role Fit Your Driver?

At parties, people often ask, "what do you do?" They never ask, "why do you do it?" Most of us identify ourselves by the work we do. Our work defines who we are and what we have accomplished. We associate with titles. Our self-worth is often connected to those titles.

If you ask people why they work, some people might answer "to make a living" or "to earn money." That answer, of course, points to the need to have an income. Often, they're earning it the best way they can. Sometimes these people do what they most enjoy outside of work.

Other people might give different answers. For example, you might hear them describe how important it is "to create something useful," "to be productive," "to contribute to a team," "to do something worthwhile," "to learn and grow," "to be admired." There are as many diverse answers as the number of people you ask. These types of answers are often linked to a person's driver – why they choose to do what they do, and why their work has meaning for them.

It's interesting that the same job can be liked or disliked by different people. Even more interesting is that the same job can be satisfying to different people for different reasons. A consultant with the Drive for Achievement may enjoy having challenging revenue targets to meet. Another consultant with a Drive for Affiliation may enjoy the client-service aspect of the job. A third one, with a Drive for Autonomy, may enjoy solving problems and developing complex project plans. Any one of these consultants might become disengaged if the focus of their business became imbalanced toward one driver over the others. Too much emphasis on billings would probably disengage those consultants who believe that either following standard practices or delivering good client service would suffer with a focus on hitting revenue targets. Conversely, too much emphasis on service or work accuracy would disengage those who believe wasted time prevents them from achieving financial goals.

So, What Does This Have to Do with Leadership?

I previously described a leader as someone who others choose to follow. To get others to follow, you need to engage them and inspire their commitment. Engaged and committed people bring more energy and drive to the work they do.

You now know that people have different motivational drivers. People are engaged by different things. That's important to know when you need to influence someone and gain their commitment. There have probably been many times when someone didn't agree with you because they had a different perspective. You may have thought to yourself, "They're ridiculous; they just don't get it. They have no idea what they're talking about." Maybe you felt upset, anxious, irritated, even angry. Why didn't they see the value of your point of view, the importance of your plan, the reasons for your objective? There will always be people who don't see things your way. However, understanding another person's driver – what's important to them – allows you to adjust the way you communicate so that they get the importance of something from their perspective, not just yours.

Part One: Relationship Acuity Insights

Leadership also requires understanding your strengths and your limitations. When you know your own driver, you are better able to recognize your potential blind spots. A blind spot is the natural tendency to focus attention only on those things that, from your perspective, are most important and ignore the things that aren't. Each driver has blind spots that are rooted in the other two drivers. Effective leadership requires you to be mindful of these blind spots.

I worked with a client organization during the financial crisis of 2008. They had just merged with another company and were suddenly faced with having to cut costs. In his message to the organization, the CEO focused on the critical need to cut people in order to ensure the financial viability of the company going forward. The message had a clear focus on results and reason – on what was happening and why. However, his message failed to acknowledge the value of the long-serving employees from both companies that were about to lose their jobs. It was a missed opportunity to engage everyone who was moving forward with the new organization. By not addressing the concerns of those with a focus on relationships, he managed to disengage a good number of those employees right from the start.

In leadership, it's important to recognize the value that all three drivers bring to a team and organization. All drivers are necessary. Work needs to get done in a timely way, healthy relationships improve productivity, and rational thinking is required in our age of information and technology. Rather than dwell on the problems that stem from their differences, it's best to focus on the creativity and new ways of thinking that the differences can inspire. When you look at things from a different perspective, fresh ideas emerge. A balanced perspective is the architect of all progress.

Nina Simone sang this great line: "I'm just a soul whose intentions are good... please don't let me be misunderstood." Good intentions are all too often misread. How often have you assumed something about someone and later discovered that you'd jumped to an inaccurate conclusion? By the same token, have others ever misunderstood your good intentions? Misunderstandings come from incorrect assumptions of intent. It happens naturally because we each look at people from our own perspective. Consider how often your perspective makes you assume bad intent before you understand the reason behind a person's words or behaviours. Remember the flow diagram in Part One. The intent behind each person's behaviour flows from their intrinsic driver. There is always a reason behind what someone does or says. Misjudging their intent can fracture a relationship. That's something no leader can afford to have happen. The first step toward preventing this problem is to be mindful that it exists. Then, try to differentiate the perceived behaviours from your assumptions of intent. That mindfulness will serve you well.

- When someone doesn't return your calls, that's the perceived behaviour. When you say to yourself, "He doesn't want to talk to me," that's your assumption about why he didn't call.

- When someone doesn't say anything in response, that's the perceived behaviour. When you say to yourself, "She's clearly not interested in what I have to say," that's your assumption about why she didn't respond.

- When you are not invited to attend a meeting, that's the perceived behaviour. When you say to yourself, "They obviously didn't want me there," that's your assumption about why you weren't invited.

In each statement, the first part is the perceived behaviour. The second part is the assumption about why that behaviour occurred. Because you can't see someone's driver, the only way to truly understand their intent is to ask them what it is. Without knowing why they're doing what they're doing, all you can do is make a guess, which will rarely be even close to the truth.

Also, if you can't see another person's intent, it goes without saying that others cannot see yours. They don't know what drives you. They won't understand why you see something one way if they don't share the same view. They will likely misjudge you. If you have the Drive for Achievement, you might push a project forward at full speed because you see the value in accomplishing the task quickly and effectively. Others might view your approach as haphazard, reckless, or uncaring. If you have the Drive for Affiliation, you might want to take the time to engage with people to better understand their needs. Others might perceive your behaviour as a waste of time or focused too much on social interactions. If you have the Drive for Autonomy, you might need to think things through before making any important decision. Others

Part One: Relationship Acuity Insights

may perceive your behaviour as lacking energy or being too slow to act. When you help people understand your underlying intent, you can prevent the assumptions that can damage a relationship.

Sometimes you might perceive someone doing something that you believe is absolutely the wrong thing to do. Remember, that's just your perspective. It's common to assume that everyone sees the world the way you do. Why wouldn't they see it my way... I'm right! When others see things the way you do – everything's great! You probably work most productively with people who see things your way. As for the others ...well, those relationships are probably your most challenging ones.

That's why understanding the essential role of perception in leadership is your next insight.

THE PERCEPTION CONNECTION

"The belief that one's own view of reality is the only reality is the most dangerous of all delusions."
—Paul Watzlawick

Many studies of emotional and social intelligence point to the importance of being able to see things from someone else's point of view. Yet if you look at the index of most leadership books, there aren't many references to perception. Why hasn't the concept of perception been further explored as a critical component of leadership? I can't answer that question, but this chapter intends to correct that oversight.

I think of perception as a leadership asset. Like any asset, you want to retain its value. To get a return on your investment of time in learning about this asset, you must become more mindful of your perceptions and frequently question why you see things the way you do. When you stop questioning, this asset becomes a liability – it can prevent you from getting the best results in your work relationships.

Perception Is *Your* Reality, Not *Theirs*

There's a difference between perception and reality. That's because perception is more than the physical act of seeing. It represents our personal interpretation of a situation. Remember those times when a colleague or boss didn't understand your point of view or your take on an issue? That happened because *your* reality was how you saw it. How they saw it was *their* reality. And if you'd compared the two realities, you'd have seen that they were probably quite different.

There's truth in the adage *seeing is believing*. Although perception depends largely upon our senses, we are always filtering and modifying what we see and hear. We believe what we see because our beliefs act as an information filter. Consider the optical illusion shown here. Do you see a face or the word Liar? Ask a few people to look at it. What do they see first?

Source: 123Optical Illusions.com

Part One: Relationship Acuity Insights

Note the differences. Once you've seen it one way, you may need someone else to help you see it a different way.

Perception creates personal perspectives. And differences in perspectives are usually the reason that work relationships can be a challenge. Each person perceives a situation and context in their own way. They don't believe that others might see it differently. They assume they share a common understanding with everyone around them until an issue becomes critical. That's when divergent viewpoints create conflict. Conflict stems primarily from different perceptions of the same situation. Different beliefs, values, and priorities lead to judgments that are often based on missing information. We each see things through our own narrow lens. We filter out additional information. There's usually much more to learn, yet we don't make an effort to look for more. We don't know what we don't know. Think about situations in your work environment where, if each side in a disagreement took the time to understand what the other side perceives and why, they might find common ground. Sometimes, if you look to a deeper level, both sides actually want the same thing. They just have different perspectives on how to get there.

Our Reality Is Just an Illusion

Our personal perspective represents what we each believe to be true. When someone speaks loudly, are they angry or just trying to be heard? If someone is quick to offer help, are they interfering or being supportive? If someone suddenly becomes quiet, are they uninterested or just thinking? The answer to each question is... it depends on the perceiver.

There is a gap between how you see yourself (your intentions) and how another person sees you (their perception). Every word and action that they hear and see is interpreted through their personal filter and forms their perception. And vice versa. That's why it's so important to make sense of what we perceive.

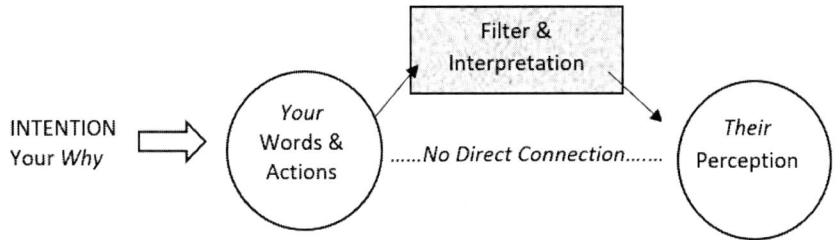

You cannot see another person's intent, and they cannot see yours. Intentions are invisible. You have no idea why a person appears unreasonable or stubborn in your eyes. You can only assume, based on what you believe to be true. And that's a problem.

The Problem with Assumptions

Assumptions fill your brain with information that is not necessarily objective or realistic.

Are you surprised when others don't agree with your perspective? When it happens, do you conclude that you're right and they're wrong? They must have a distorted view of the world, or else they would see things your way, right? Think about the assumptions you make on a regular basis. These assumptions distort your picture of someone else's reality. I once worked with a team of systems developers. Everyone on the team valued taking extra time to produce the best quality work. They assumed that their clients were willing to overlook missed deadlines as long as they received a good product in the end. But that assumption was wrong. Their clients complained about all the frustrating delays. It's not that they didn't value quality work, but they also needed the work delivered on time!

It is quite common for managers to assume they know what their employees want, usually because it reflects what they themselves would want. That's their perspective, not the perspective of the people on their team.

These faulty assumptions can often result in disengaged and disgruntled employees who are rewarded in meaningless ways. My client Ron provides a good example of this. Ron was an exceptional salesperson and his company decided to reward his strong performance by promoting him to a management position. At the time, Ron saw this promotion as a dilemma, not a reward. He didn't really want the management job.

Part One: Relationship Acuity Insights

He preferred meeting with his customers. His customer relationships contributed to his sales results. Ron knew that turning down a promotion would not be well-received, so he accepted the role. To his credit, he lasted two years in a job he didn't enjoy. Then he was dismissed for poor performance. Unfortunately, this is often how companies unwittingly transform exceptional performers into unexceptional ones. They take a person out of a job they enjoy and put them into one they don't. Ron was successful in sales because his sense of purpose was rooted in his passion for working with his clients. In his new role, he was required to manage the people who were doing the job he loved. Ron eventually returned to a sales position, but only after a difficult process of persuading future employers that he was, in fact, a success, not a failure.

This story could have had a better ending. Not only did Ron lose his job, but his company lost their best salesperson. Rather than assuming that Ron wanted the more senior role, the outcome could have been quite different had his boss first asked him what he valued about his job, why he was so good at it, and what he would consider a meaningful reward. This was the information that was critically needed to engage and retain someone who was a high performer.

We can all think back to at least a few times when our assumptions have been wrong and we've suffered a consequence for it. The good news is that assumptions, once identified, can be revised and corrected.

Assumptions Create Illusions of Certainty

Akira Kurosawa's 1950 psychological drama *The Rashomon Effect* highlights the idea that certainty about something becomes almost impossible when there are many different and opposing perspectives. In the film, each person interpreted an incident based on their perception of it. They didn't realize that their perception was influenced by what they *believed* to be true, that it was subjective. As a result, people had difficulty verifying what was true and what was an illusion of the truth.

If you want something to be true, you believe it to be true. Unfortunately, this belief can lead you to stop looking further. You stop gathering information when the evidence you've gathered confirms your own views. Your lens narrows and you might no longer perceive circumstances objectively. You might block out options and fill in the blanks. It's important to recognize this tendency to *filter in* and *filter out* information. Look no further than today's partisan politics to see this same phenomenon. Opposing sides each have firm beliefs about what is right and what is wrong. Neither side listens to the other and neither side attempts to gain a different perspective.

In his book *Thinking, Fast and Slow*, psychologist Daniel Kahneman looks at the two ways our minds process the interpersonal information we receive. Kahneman discovered that we perceive each other in two distinct systems of reasoning. "System One" processes information quickly, intuitively, and automatically. I refer to this as being in a stage of *unconscious thinking*. It's effortless, like driving down a familiar road where you can let your mind wander and still arrive at your intended destination. Or when you assume someone agrees with you because you see them nod and smile. This shortcut in thinking leads to incorrect assumptions and conclusions. Jim Acosta, author of *The Enemy of the People: A Dangerous Time to Tell the Truth in America*, once reported in an interview that he believed the greatest danger in today's world was that people would get their news only from those information sources that shared their point of view. In a sense, Acosta was pointing to the danger of operating only under System One, where our minds are closed to seeing things from a different perspective.

By contrast, Kahneman's "System Two" is our more deliberate method of processing information. This processing takes a little more effort and mental energy because we must become mindful of the situation. I refer to this as moving to a stage of *conscious thinking*. We are aware that we need more information to help us interpret what we are seeing. It's like driving in a foreign city with unfamiliar roads, or noticing an odd facial expression that makes us wonder what the person is thinking and why.

We see evidence of System Two when we consider our tendency toward confirmation bias. First described by psychologist Peter Wason, confirmation bias supports the premise that people are, by nature, prone to believing what they want to believe. It isn't in our nature to look for evidence to disprove our beliefs. We tend to seek out further information that supports those beliefs. Confirmation bias explains why strong opinions grow even stronger. We filter in only information that supports our beliefs and filter out information that doesn't.

Corporate recruiters often experience confirmation bias, unwittingly allowing first impressions to determine the outcomes of their hiring decisions. Two sides of this phenomenon are sometimes called the halo effect (an interviewer's tendency to initially overestimate a candidate's value if they see something early in the interview that they believe is a positive quality) and the horns effect (the interviewer's tendency to stop looking for positives once they've seen what they believe is a negative factor). Once a candidate creates an impression, either positive or negative, the interviewer subconsciously looks for confirming evidence to support their initial belief.

A corporate recruiter once told me about her experiences with this form of bias. From the moment she would greet a candidate, her perceptions were filtered by her own personal values and expectations. She would judge whether their handshake was strong or weak and whether they appeared polite or seemed warm and friendly. Her initial beliefs influenced her decision to move those candidates forward in the process or not. Only those candidates that met her personal criteria made it through to the next stage. Most often, her decisions were based solely on her opinions, not objective data related to the role. On reflection, she felt sure that she had mistakenly screened out a lot of qualified candidates because she filtered out important information. Had she been aware of this bias, she would have looked not only for confirming evidence but for contrary evidence as well.

It's a good idea to be aware of this natural tendency to filter what you see and judge as right or wrong, good or bad, or true or false. Then consciously look for information that provides new information and insight. A fresh perspective is a powerful way to shift how you see things, including what you believe to be true and how to respond to different people in different circumstances.

"If Only You Could See It *My* Way"

When someone says, "Look at it this way," what they really mean is, "Look at it *my* way." We all want people to see things our way. When they don't, we feel upset, anxious, or irritated. If this has happened to you, maybe you thought that if you talked louder, they would understand where you were coming from. Unfortunately, that's like going to a country where others don't speak your language and just speaking more slowly and loudly in the hopes of being understood.

This is a fundamental leadership challenge because it's about your ability to be influential. There will always be people who see things differently than you do, based on what *they* value. Being able to influence someone who has a different perspective is a critical skill to have. If you're frustrated by someone who apparently just doesn't get it, take the opportunity to step back and allow yourself to be open to seeing things through different eyes. If you look at things only through your eyes, it's like looking into a mirror. You're only getting a reflection of yourself!

I met Bill, a senior operations executive, in an impromptu coaching session. Bill was someone who needed to see things from a different perspective. I was asked to speak with him about an alleged "bullying" incident with one of his employees. I asked Bill to share what he said to the employee who lodged the complaint.

As I listened to his recounting of the discussion (which involved a performance issue he had to address with the employee), I found Bill's words and tone of voice to be somewhat threatening. I shared that perception with him, and he was astonished. He couldn't understand what I found threatening about his words. He was giving honest feedback, he said, and that's how he would expect feedback to be given to him. He had real difficulty understanding how his message could be perceived differently by someone else.

This leads to the question, was Bill's approach wrong? Some people would say yes, but others might agree with his approach. Was I right in my perception of his behaviour? In my opinion, yes. But others might not agree. Those who don't appreciate "soft" feedback might be annoyed if someone tried to deliver a gentle message to avoid hurting their feelings. They would much prefer direct, honest words, with no holding back. Had Bill delivered that same message to someone like that, there may not have been a complaint in the first place.

This is a common leadership dilemma. People perceive messages in different ways, depending on what they value. A message you would value receiving might not be received in the same way by someone else. Bill didn't realize that what he said and how he said it could determine the positive or negative impact of his message. Delivering that message to someone like himself would have gotten the result he wanted – appreciation for the feedback. But his employee had a different perspective and his message was perceived as bullying rather than productive. It's best to try to understand your audience and consider how your words and actions might be perceived. When having an important conversation, it's wise to first ask yourself, "How might this person see this situation differently, and how might they react?"

Actions Always Speak Louder Than Words

We all act out of habit based on what we believe is the right thing to do. Have you ever stopped to think that maybe a different way of approaching someone might get you a better result? You may have walked away from a situation and wondered why things didn't go as well as planned. Before entering into that interaction, had you considered what your audience valued? Whether they would understand your intent? The fact is, what you did or said may have worked in a different scenario, but different situations almost always require that you consider the most effective approach at that moment.

The good news is that we always have the power to choose a different action and reaction. We just have to be mindful and open to new learning. Paul Watzlawick, a psychotherapist and philosopher, is noted for having said, "you cannot <u>not</u> communicate." Every interaction we have with someone is a form of communication that is perceived. Perception is a result of each person's interpretations of the meaning behind the words and actions they hear and see. Then, automatic judgments are formed. For example:

- If you have the Drive for Achievement, you might judge someone who takes time to think before acting to be slow or indecisive.

- If you have the Drive for Affiliation, you might judge someone who speaks sharply to another to be heartless or uncaring.

- If you have the Drive for Autonomy, you might judge someone who constantly socializes with colleagues to lack focus or be inattentive to the task at hand.

We have all heard the term *walk the talk*. It's another way of saying be authentic – do what you say you'll do, so that people will see you doing it. I've always believed that there's a bit of a problem with this. Even when you intend to be authentic, others will interpret your behaviour in their own way, sometimes quite differently from the way you intended it. They can't see your purpose or your intent. They can only assume. Very often, when different people look at the same thing, they interpret what they see in different ways – the Rashomon effect.

This further explains why perception is so important when we talk about leadership. Each person has their own interpretation of what they see. You say or do something that feels right to you, but there's a strong likelihood that others perceive and interpret it differently. The classic example of this is the glass half-empty or half-full analogy.

Let's go further with this concept. Heteronyms are a great example. You may not be familiar with the term heteronym, but you've surely experienced them in written communication. Heteronyms are words that are spelled the same but have different meanings when pronounced differently. When you read a word without any additional information, you immediately assume its pronunciation and meaning based on your own perception. Here are some examples:

Lead: Verb – *to guide*; Noun – *a metal*
Alternate: Verb – *to switch back and forth*; Noun – *another choice*
Conduct: Verb – *to lead*; Noun – *behaviour*
Attribute: Verb – *to consider something as resulting from*; Noun – *a characteristic*
Record: Verb – *to keep in permanent form*; Noun – *a written or verbal account*

Show someone each word outside the context of a sentence and ask them to tell you what each word means and how they would pronounce it. Note the differences in response.

Change Perception, Change *Everything*

I once mediated a conflict between a sales manager and his director. The sales manager was charged with introducing a new, scaled-back bonus system to his team. He was uncomfortable having to tell his team about it because it meant a significant drop in commissions. He understood the business rationale for the change, but he also knew his team would not be pleased. To mitigate the impact, he communicated the message to his team in a way that showed his support for them and their feelings. Soon, word got back to the director that the sales manager didn't actually support the new bonus system. Of course, that was not his intent. The director didn't understand why his manager was acting in such a disrespectful way. He assumed that the manager's intent was to undermine his business decision. Assumptions like this can be costly. Luckily he spoke with the manager and learned his true intent, avoiding what could have been an expensive and unnecessary termination. The director didn't agree with his manager's approach, but he did understand why his manager did what he did. That understanding opened the door to an agreement about how to keep their relationship productive.

The moral of this story is this: when you see someone doing something you find confusing or conflicting, pause. Find out if you have all the information. Ask for the other person's perspective. Find out their *why*. There's only one way to understand what drives a person's behaviour, and that's to ask them. Without knowing *why*, all you're doing is making an uneducated guess.

It's Not All Them. Sometimes It's *You*

You are harder to understand than you may realize. Many of us think we're veritable open books to everyone around us. You might believe others know what you know – your thoughts and your intentions. Social psychologist and author Heidi Grant-Halvorson conducts research on how people make sense of one another. Her research supports the fact that, in any interaction, you are the only one who knows your intentions, your thoughts, and your feelings. Others can only hear your words and observe your behaviour. From that, they assume your reasons why.

Given the many obstacles to accurate perception, how can you be sure to come across as you intend? For one thing, you need to send clear signals about your intentions. When you do, it's more likely that others will understand you and see you the way you see yourself. Be sure to share your perspective and let them know your *why*.

Now, Pause for Insight

It's time to reflect on the insight you have gained in Part One of this book. This focus has been on the impact of two key factors on your work relationships: your intrinsic driver (your *why*) and your perceptions. Be mindful of these two factors. They ultimately guide how you act and interact with others. And the quality of your interactions largely determines your effectiveness as a leader.

Part Two shows how these factors relate to the twelve Relationship Acuity competencies – the behaviours that form the building blocks of leadership.

Part Two:
Relationship Acuity Competencies

Relationship Acuity Competencies are Differentiators

> *"People are hired for technical competence,*
> *fired for their interpersonal incompetence,*
> *and promoted for their leadership skills."*
> —Jack Zenger/Joseph Folkman

Let's look at how the concepts presented in Part One fit together to influence your leadership capabilities. If you are confused or conflicted by what you see people doing, then you need to learn why they are doing what they do. That's the only way you're going to develop a different perspective. This might help you to see someone with whom you have a difficult working relationship in a totally different light. For the most part, no one sets out to intentionally do what they believe is the wrong thing. They are doing it with a purpose in mind. It's up to you to find out what that purpose is before you make a faulty assumption and pass judgment on their actions. Then consider what you can do in response to it, to make your relationship work.

Sometimes, based on our perceptions, we are driven to respond to situations and people in ways that work against our intent. Think of a time when you didn't agree with what you saw happening around you or what you heard being said. You may have responded in a way that had you later asking yourself, "Why didn't I wait before I opened my mouth?" or, "Why didn't I speak up instead of remaining silent?" or, "Why did I just give in, when I totally disagreed?" When this happens, many people use their "personality" as an excuse for their actions. They may say to themselves, "That's just me. Not much I can do about it. People need to accept me for who I am." If you're saying these things, it tells me that you're not willing to change and that you think you have no choice.

The reality is that you do have a choice.

This leads us to the concept of personal and interpersonal competencies. In the past, it was assumed that a person's intelligence or degree of knowledge, skill, and experience was the best predictor of job performance. Then, in the early '70s, David McClelland, a psychologist based at Harvard University, introduced the concept of competencies.

Competencies focus on what an outstanding performer does that gets better results than an average performer. They include skills and

53

Part Two: Relationship Acuity Competencies

behaviours. A competency represents an overall ability, skills refer to the execution of that ability, and behaviours are how others observe those skills. Within each competency are specific skills and behaviours that can be learned.

McClelland's work on competencies was a turning point in the leadership development industry. Organizations now generate competency lists in the assessment of leadership potential. These competencies often define the skills needed to achieve management objectives. They focus on *what* a leader should be able to do to achieve goals and objectives. Given what we've covered so far, I would add that it is also important to focus on *how* that leader behaves when working with others.

This brings us to the difference between leadership and management.

Many years ago, an instructor from the Royal Military College of Canada was a guest speaker in my organization's management development program. He asked the class to consider what the difference was between management and leadership. There were a few responses, after which he shared that the military has a very simple way of differentiating between the two terms: "In war time you can always *lead* a man to his death, but you can never *manage* a man to his death." While management focuses on the tasks a person is required to do, leadership includes an interpersonal component with a focus on how people relate to one another.

Harvard Business School professor John Kotter further clarifies that management and leadership are different but complementary. In his view, one can't effectively function without the other. This is a key point. Management is about implementing systems and processes that make an organization function well. It includes planning, budgeting, organizing, and controlling. In contrast, leadership encompasses the concepts of energy, empowerment, motivation, and inspiration. It's about enabling people to behave in different ways in order to get better outcomes.

And yet, business schools remain focused more on the development of managers and less on the development of leaders. Research supports this premise. Greg Patton, a professor at the Marshall School of Business at the University of Southern California, noted at a 2012 conference that "the challenge of today's business schools is to develop MBAs who are also excellent leaders of people." If you get an MBA, you may have technical skills, but are you able to lead people?

Relationship Acuity Competencies are Differentiators

In their July 2018 Harvard Business Review article "Self-Awareness Can Help Leaders More Than an MBA Can," authors Rasmus Hougaard, Jacqueline Carter, and Marissa Afton compile the results of several large-scale studies. These studies found that "leadership based solely on MBA-trained logic is... often detrimental to an organization's productivity. If the linear MBA-trained logic becomes the sole focus — at the cost of other skills, like self-awareness and understanding others and the culture — the leadership approach is out of balance."

Leadership Competencies Are Relationship-Based

Leadership competencies don't replace the important management competencies that have been identified over the years. Leadership competencies work hand-in-hand with management and technical skills. They become even more important as you climb to the higher rungs on your career ladder. Bill George, professor of leadership at Harvard Business School, has referred to self-awareness as the "starting point" of leadership. Through self-awareness we are better at leading ourselves and others.

Relationship Acuity competencies are laser-focused on leadership. They are critical for any role you acquire in any organization. When you learn and apply them, you are well on your way to eliminating up to 90% of the people problems that many consultants and coaches are hired to fix. These competencies are even more critical today, as organizations are dealing with increasing diversity and rapid change while trying to remain productive and profitable.

Relationship building is the cornerstone of leadership success. If you learn, reflect on, and practice the skills within these competencies, you will truly see the difference! Instead of spending time and energy dealing with the problems that come from unhealthy work relationships, you will have more time and energy to spend on creating opportunities for yourself and your team. Be mindful of the impact your actions have on others. Work to better understand others in terms of what inspires them. Doing so earns trust, mutual respect, loyalty, commitment, and active engagement. Now that's worth working on!

THE TWELVE BUILDING BLOCKS OF LEADERSHIP

"We could learn a lot from crayons; some are sharp, some are pretty, some are dull, while others bright, some have weird names, but they all have learned to live together in the same box."—Robert Fulghum

In a box of crayons, you look inside to find the different colours available to you. Similarly, in the box of Relationship Acuity, there are twelve competencies available to use and practice that, together, serve to sharpen your acuity in your relationships. They are the building blocks for growing into an effective leader over the course of your career, from entry-level to management, and ultimately to the senior levels of an organization.

The foundation of this box of competencies is the **personal leadership** level – the entry point of your career. At this level, you are the sole contributor. There are five competencies at this level that, together, help you **develop personal and interpersonal effectiveness**.

The second level represents a move into a **team leadership** role. There are an additional five Team Leadership competencies that, together, allow you to **achieve results through others**.

The third level is reached at the senior executive ranks in an **organizational leadership** role. At this most senior level, you need to apply all of the previous competencies, plus two that specifically facilitate your ability to **generate corporate energy**.

The twelve Relationship Acuity competencies, shown in the diagram on the next page, form a structure of personal and interpersonal leadership competence. Before we dive into the individual competencies, let's review each level of leadership. As you review them, consider your current competence at the level that is appropriate for you.

LEADERSHIP BUILDING BLOCKS

Sharpen Acuity in Your Relationships

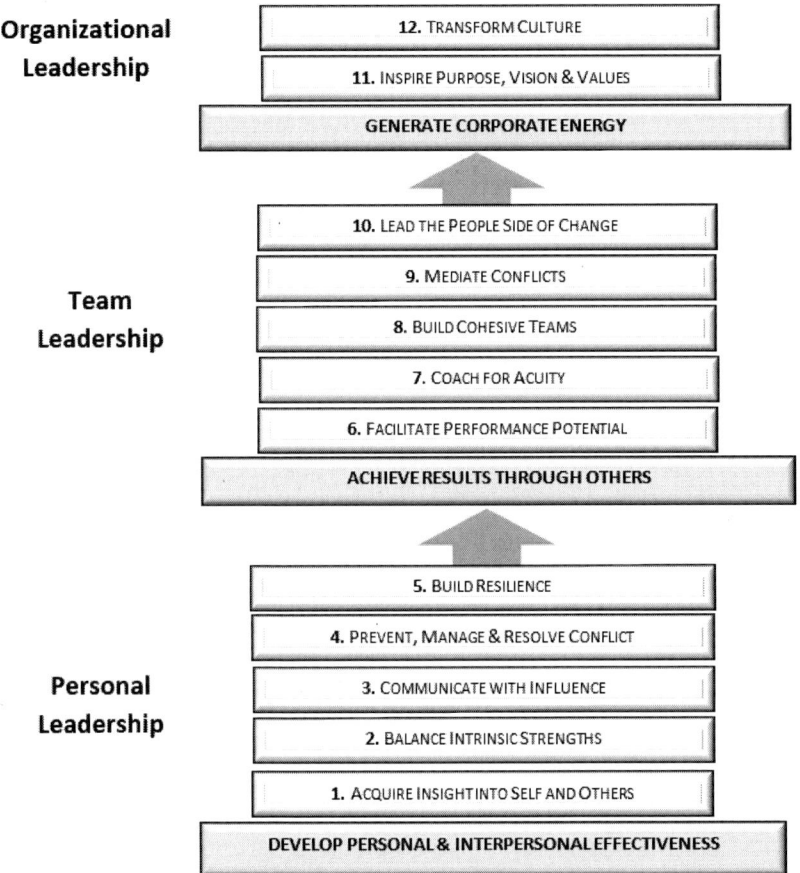

Part Two: Relationship Acuity Competencies

Level 1: Personal Leadership: Building Productive Relationships

It goes without saying, but I'll say it anyway: you need to lead yourself before you can lead others. All leadership starts at this level. You don't need to be in a position of authority to be considered a leader, but you do need to be influential when working with others.

When you're an individual contributor, no one reports directly to you. But you still need to interact with a lot of people each and every day: your boss, your colleagues, internal or external customers and clients, individuals in other functional areas, and others.

These people are all in what I call your *sphere of influence*. Your sphere of influence includes those people to whom you are connected in some capacity in your role. They represent your most important work relationships, people necessary to interact with to do your job. These are all important relationships and you will need to consider how to make each one more productive. As you work through the Personal Leadership competencies, always keep the people in that sphere in mind.

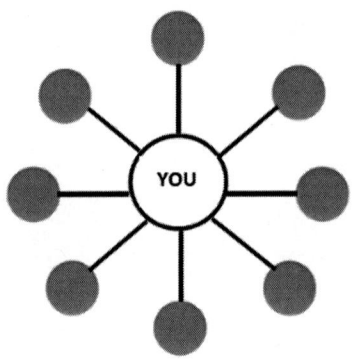

Consider Your Competence as a Personal Leader

The following statements reflect Relationship Acuity at the personal leadership level. Check those that apply to you.

- ☐ I know what drives my behaviour and feeds my self-worth
- ☐ I can identify a sense of purpose in my work that engages me and gives me energy to do my best
- ☐ I place a high value on the quality of my work relationships
- ☐ I can name the people who represent my most important work relationships
- ☐ I understand what's important to the people in my work relationships – what they value most

☐ I ensure that people in my work relationships understand what's important to me – what I value most
☐ I believe my personal and interpersonal effectiveness is critical to achieving success in my career
☐ I know how to prevent potential conflicts with the key people in my sphere of influence
☐ I know how to manage and resolve conflicts when they occur
☐ I know how to relate differently with different people, in different situations, for better outcomes
☐ I always get my intended results in productive ways when I interact with others
☐ I respond to setbacks in proactive ways that reduce stress and improve my productivity

Did you check at least seven? If so, that's great – you are already operating at quite a good level of personal leadership. There's always room for improvement, but this is a great start. If you didn't check more than seven, that's okay, too. That's why you're reading this book. In either case, after reviewing and practicing the Personal Leadership competencies, revisit this list and see if you are able to check off more.

Level 2: Team Leadership: *Developing Engaged People*

Once you become a team leader, you are no longer responsible just for yourself. You are responsible for the performance of the members of your team. I refer to your direct reports as *associates* rather than employees. The word *associate* best implies a collaborative partnership with the people who support you in achieving your goals and objectives.

While at this point, you still need to manage the relationships in your sphere of influence, you now need to further understand the people who report directly to you. What drives each of them? What do they care about? What strengths do they each bring to the team? What weaknesses need to be addressed?

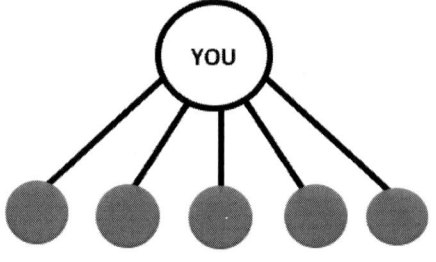

Part Two: Relationship Acuity Competencies

With this knowledge, you are better able to clarify expectations, provide meaningful feedback and rewards, develop high-performance potential, and keep your team engaged and cohesive.

Consider Your Competence as a Team Leader

The following statements reflect Relationship Acuity at the team leadership level. Check those that apply to you.

- ☐ I make sure each of my associates is aware of what I value and what drives me
- ☐ I know each of my associates in terms of what they value and what drives them
- ☐ I encourage each associate to understand how their role links to their sense of purpose
- ☐ I am confident in my ability to help each associate achieve their performance potential
- ☐ I recognize and reward my highest performing associates in ways that matter most to them
- ☐ I maintain objectivity when providing feedback to each associate
- ☐ I am mindful of the impact of my perceptions when judging the behaviours of my associates
- ☐ I solicit feedback regarding how others view my effectiveness as the team leader
- ☐ I am confident in my ability to help associates deal with personal or interpersonal issues
- ☐ I know how to build and sustain a cohesive and engaged team
- ☐ I believe it is important that relationships on my team remain healthy and productive
- ☐ When trust is low on the team, I work at building it back up
- ☐ I know how to prevent conflict on my team
- ☐ I know how to mediate conflicts between my associates
- ☐ I know how to reduce stress and maintain productivity during major change initiatives

The Twelve Building Blocks of Leadership

Did you check at least eight? If so, you're already on the right track. If not, you'll have plenty of opportunities to practice and improve as you work through this book. After reviewing and practicing the Team Leadership competencies, revisit this list and see if you're able to check off more.

Level 3: Organizational Leadership: *Creating an Inspired Culture*

Once you join the group of senior leaders charged with the stewardship of your organization, you are collectively working as an executive team focused on the well-being of all of your stakeholders and of the organization as a whole.

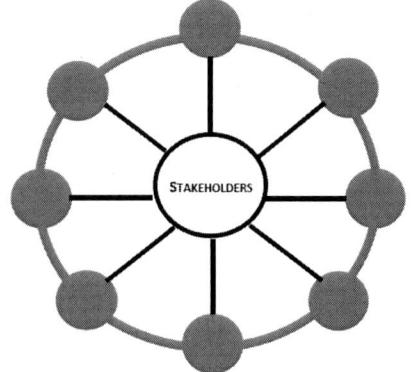

You are now at the highest level of influence. You are both a functional/operational leader and a strategic leader. While maintaining relationships within your own sphere of influence and managing those with your direct reports, you are now also required to work within a group of interdependent strategic leaders.

Your challenge here is to move from the perception of a *siloed* model to a *systemic* interdependent model. More than ever, this requires managing many diverse relationships – *up* (your boss, or the board if you're the CEO), *across* (your colleagues), and *down* (your associates). As a collective group, your team must both create and live the culture of your organization. Every day, your focus must be to demonstrate your organization's values in everything you do. This is much more difficult than it appears. Your perceptions continue to influence your unique perspective on how you demonstrate those values.

Part Two: Relationship Acuity Competencies

Consider Your Competence as an Organizational Leader

The following statements represent Relationship Acuity at the organizational leadership level. Check those that apply to you.

- ☐ I understand the importance of influence as an organizational leader
- ☐ I value a systems-thinking perspective when looking at my role as an organizational leader
- ☐ I have a vision of what a high-functioning leadership team looks like and have shared that vision with the team
- ☐ I believe in the importance of cohesion on a senior leadership team and frequently check that our team is cohesive, as well as aligned
- ☐ I am mindful about shifting from a functional leadership perspective to a broader stewardship perspective that guides the culture of the organization
- ☐ I believe it is important for our team to define and create a desired team culture
- ☐ I frequently remind myself and my colleagues that we are not only functional leaders, but also stewards of our organization
- ☐ I am vigilant and call attention to the risks to our credibility when we don't behave in ways that demonstrate our organization's culture and values
- ☐ I endeavour to maintain continuous open and frank dialogue on critical team and organizational issues
- ☐ I attempt to prevent, not avoid, interpersonal conflict within our team and encourage others to do the same

Did you check at least six? If not, it's entirely normal. Maybe you're not in a senior leadership role yet. And even if you are, it's rare to find leaders already operating at this level. You've made the right choice in reading this book and committing to improving. You'll get there! After reviewing and practicing the Organizational Leadership competencies, revisit this list and see if you are able to check off more.

PERSONAL LEADERSHIP COMPETENCIES

Develop Personal and Interpersonal Effectiveness

"Be yourself. Everyone else is already taken."
—Oscar Wilde

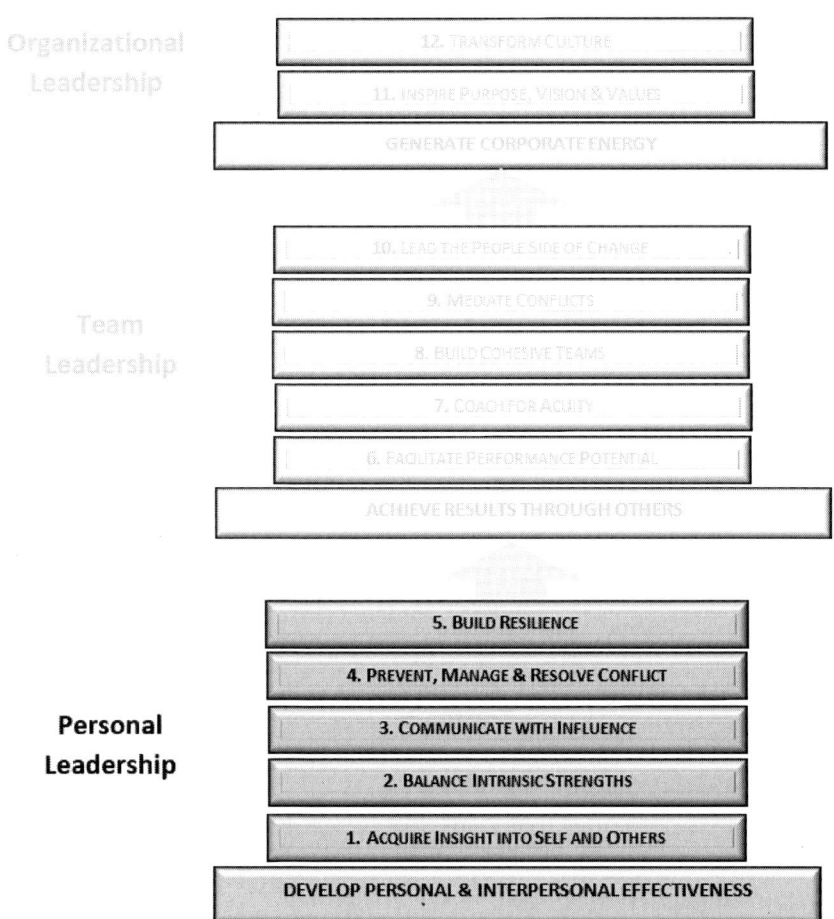

Part Two: Personal Leadership Competencies

Leaders Must Demonstrate Personal and Interpersonal Effectiveness

"The most basic of all human needs is the need to understand and be understood." —Ralph Nichols

Productive relationships happen when people understand each other.

Personal and interpersonal effectiveness is grounded in the power of communicating with people in mutually beneficial ways. It's about ensuring that each person is understood. When that happens, you build healthy and productive relationships. Developing personal and interpersonal effectiveness starts with understanding what drives your own behaviour and the behaviour of others – why people do what they do.

You need to be understood by others. When someone understands you, they are more likely to listen to what you have to say and be willing to engage with you.

To help the people you work with understand you, you must first understand yourself at a deeper level. Can you answer the following questions?

- What drives your behaviour? What's your *why?*

- How do you see yourself? What do you believe are your strengths and your weaknesses?

- Do others see you the way you see yourself? If not, why not?

- Do you look at things the same way others do, or do you believe other people are "out to lunch?"

You need to understand others. When you understand another person, you are more likely to listen to what they have to say and be willing to engage with them.

To understand the people you work with, you must go further than assumptions and seek to understand them at a deeper level. Can you answer the following questions?

- What drives their behaviour? What's their why?

Demonstrate Personal and Interpersonal Effectiveness

- How do they see themselves? What do they believe are their strengths and weaknesses?

- Do you see others the way they see themselves? If not, why not?

- Do they look at things the same way you do, or do they believe you are "out to lunch"?

There are five competencies that contribute to the development of personal and interpersonal effectiveness. Let's look at each in detail.

COMPETENCY #1: Acquire Insight Into Self and Others

> *"Even though self-awareness – knowing who we are and how we're seen – is important for job performance, career success, and leadership effectiveness, it's in remarkably short supply in today's workplace. In our nearly five-year research program on the subject, we've discovered that although 95% of people think they're self-aware, only 10 to 15% actually are."*
> —Tasha Eurich

Think of the people you work with every day who, in your opinion, lack self-awareness. You walk away from a conversation and you think it's too bad they have no idea how they come across. It would sure be good for them to acquire some insight into how they are perceived. Similar statements are likely being uttered by the people in your sphere of influence. What might others say about you?

Insight into self and others is the most basic leadership competency. It's about developing a deeper understanding of what drives behaviour. Developing it starts with taking the time to understand yourself, then gaining a deeper understanding of others.

Look in Before You Look Out

Consider your answers to the following questions:

- How do I see myself?

- How do others see me?

- What is the difference between the two?

There are a number of tools in the learning and development field to provide the opportunity for self-insight and awareness. I believe the most insightful learning experience comes from discovering what we and others value most and then learning what to do with that information. This means looking at yourself and others through the lens of our *sense of purpose*.

COMPETENCY #1: ACQUIRE INSIGHT INTO SELF AND OTHERS

Insight into Yourself

In his book *Even Eagles Need a Push,* David McNally reminds us of the story of Terry Fox. Terry completed the greatest marathon run in history. And, of course, he did it as an amputee. McNally wanted to find out what drove Terry to run that marathon. As McNally relates, Terry discovered a purpose – a "compelling reason to live that was much more important than his own difficulties... being committed to something that transcended oneself." His purpose was to seek a cure for cancer. He became a hero because of his commitment to this sense of purpose. When you have a purpose, your actions have meaning and direction.

In Part One, you read about our drive for self-worth and our sense of purpose. Your purpose is your mission in life. It emanates from within you. When you reflect on your purpose, you are defining your value. When you are valued, you have a feeling of self-worth.

So, What's Driving You?
Research on peak performers has shown one quality they all have in common: they all have a drive for what they are passionate about doing. Passion is linked to high performance. Yet, success in our schools is still tied to the ability to memorize and apply information. Top grades are earned by students who have the skill to recall stored data. Our education system seems to believe that future success and classroom grades go hand-in-hand, and students with the best grades are labelled most likely to succeed. Yet, numerous studies have shown that grades are not necessarily the barometer of success. I have heard it said that over 50% of CEOs of Fortune 500 companies report that they earned C averages in school. In a 2007 Maclean's magazine article, journalist Sarah Scott presented findings along these lines, including the fact that Angus Reid failed high-school English and then built a successful polling business; that Winston Churchill was at the bottom of his class at Harrow; and that Richard Branson left high school to become the founder of a global business empire.

It's a sobering fact that over 70% of workers report having low job satisfaction. If you could ask that 70% why they work, it's likely, they'll tell you about their need to make money. They make money in order to do the things they love to do outside of work. These are the TGIF group.

Part Two: Personal Leadership Competencies

They love Friday and get energized as the weekend approaches. They can't wait to get out of work each day. On the other hand, there are TGIM people who look forward to Monday. Their answers about why they work might be to build an enterprise, to solve problems, to help people grow, to create effective systems, or to make things better. The list of potential answers is endless. Which group are you in? If you have low job satisfaction, ask yourself why.

When I asked a group of scientists in a global pharmaceutical company why they worked in research, I fully expected them to say they enjoyed analyzing scientific data and developing new, more effective drugs. Instead, every one of them said, in different ways, that they wanted to improve people's health and to make the world a better place. That's a different reason than just wanting to analyze data and produce formulas. Those responses changed my perception of these researchers. They weren't driven by their task, but by the potential outcome of their research – to improve people's health! This link between job satisfaction and performance is by no means a perfect science. However, think of it as a fundamental principle that demonstrates the link between passion and productivity.

In Part One of this book, we talked about how intrinsic drivers differ. You probably gained some insight into your own sense of purpose or self-worth. What did you discover about your driver – what most often inspires you to do what you do? What gives you meaning in your work? You may want to lead. You may want to follow. Maybe you want to help others or solve complex problems. You probably have a little of each driver within you, but your true sense of purpose will usually override the others. That's because when you fulfill your purpose in your work, you believe your work has meaning and your efforts are worthwhile. You feel that sense of self-worth. Do you want to make a difference in people's lives? Build a business? Become a renowned expert in a field?

Ask yourself what you believe is the purpose of your role. I don't mean your list of tasks and objectives. That's what the job requires. But why does it exist? How does it contribute to the success of your organization? Without that role, what would happen? Answers to these questions provide a sense of purpose in what you do.

COMPETENCY #1: ACQUIRE INSIGHT INTO SELF AND OTHERS

How Do Others See You?

You now hopefully have a sense of your own driver. The next step is to focus on the relationships in your sphere of influence. Which ones would you like to improve? Would you like more honest communication? Greater mutual respect? Less conflict? What might each improved relationship look like? To do this, start by learning about how other people see you. It's good to get the view of people you respect by seeking what I call relationship-based feedback. In her book *Help Them Grow or Watch Them Go: Career Conversations Employees Want*, renowned author Dr. Beverly Kaye explains the need for feedback nicely: "There is something to be learned from nearly everyone we encounter. A low feedback diet may be harmful to the health of your business. Side effects include disengagement, stunted growth, lack of clarity, lost opportunities and loss of talent."

There is usually a gap between the perception you have of yourself and the perceptions others have of you, so it's important to actively seek feedback on how you're seen by others. Remember, relationship-based feedback is different than the performance-based assessments that are integrated into an organization's performance management system. These organizational assessments are sometimes used as a punitive tool to address poor performance, not as a development tool. That's given feedback a bad rap. If your organization fosters anonymous feedback, you may have found it less helpful than intended. Covert communication without open dialogue never builds trust. I've seen reputations ruined and jobs lost as a result of this process. It takes a long time to rebuild trust in organizations that have used feedback and assessment processes in this way. People soon learn how to choose feedback providers that make them look good, rather than welcome feedback that helps them grow.

The first thing to know about relationship feedback is that it is based on perception. It's how someone sees you from a personal perspective. Relationship-based feedback comes from people you choose, and you should be very deliberate about choosing people with whom you have both productive and non-productive relationships, in order to get diverse perspectives. While you may believe you demonstrate a trusting nature, some people may perceive you to be naïve. If you see yourself as confident, others may perceive you to be arrogant. If you pride yourself on being a practical person, you may be seen to lack imagination.

Part Two: Personal Leadership Competencies

The value of relationship-based feedback cannot be underestimated. It clarifies how each person sees you from their point of view. It's a reality check that tells you that things are not always how they appear. It offers the opportunity for you and the people you work with to broaden your perspectives.

Seeking feedback is not about validating what you believe to be true about yourself. It's about having the courage to learn how you're perceived and what impact you have on others. It's good to be open to other perspectives. It shines a light on the difference between your intent and your impact.

Your feedback providers can include anyone within your sphere of influence – your boss, colleagues, clients, customers, and beyond. Proactively seeking feedback from these people gives you the opportunity to see different points of view. You can check each person's assumptions about you and, in turn, help them understand the reasons that you do what you do. That is information they may be lacking, particularly if how they see you is surprising to you. In the process, you'll discover something about them too. How you see them may not be in sync with how they see themselves either. This whole process provides an opportunity to check perspectives from both sides – yours and theirs.

Think about who your best feedback providers might be. Imagine you have the opportunity to spend some time with someone in a feedback discussion. Who would you choose, and why? What would you like to learn about their perceptions of you? What would you gain from that person's perspective? How would you use that information?

Ideally, you want to create an opportunity for an open dialogue that encourages candid and honest feedback. Everyone's time is valuable these days, so it's up to you to decide how much time you might ask of them. Obviously, the more time, the richer the discussion, but the quantity of time you request of them is less important than the quality of the feedback you receive. Also, in-person conversations are usually the best. Face-to-face communication is far more effective than an e-mail exchange. People are often reticent to write down their thoughts, and written communication has a much greater likelihood of being misinterpreted.

A few further suggestions to get the most out of your feedback providers' time:

- Always thank them for their time.

- Never argue or debate, even if you disagree with what the person has said.

- Ask clarifying questions to make sure you understand their message. The most valuable questions are those that specifically ask what you have done or not done that contributed to their seeing things the way they do.

- Ask what you should stop doing, start doing, and continue doing. Or find out the one thing they would like to see you do more of, less of, or differently.

- Remember that feedback is filtered by a person's intrinsic driver – it's only their perspective. All feedback is perception. That's why it's ideal to solicit feedback from a variety of people within your sphere of influence.

Insight into Others

If the world were a perfect place, everyone would act the way we expect them to. However, the reality is that we must accept people for who they are. We all have met people who we wish would be different. Our relationships with these people are challenging at best and toxic at worst.

Think of the people with whom you currently work. Are there some that you just don't get? No matter what your efforts, you just can't see eye to eye or connect with them in a positive way. If they're in your sphere of influence, reflect on the interactions you've had with them. Would you like to make those relationships better? If so, you can start by building acuity in your perceptions of them – specifically in terms of what they value. As I've said before, no one gets up in the morning with the intent to do the *wrong* thing. Understanding *why* someone does something is a much better strategy than judging *what* they do. Yet, every day, we see people judging others based on how they interpret what they see and hear. So, if you perceive someone doing something you don't agree with, try to think about their good intentions. Go beyond your perceptions to try to understand where they're coming from. Focus on their driver, not yours.

Avoid Judgments and Assumptions of Intent

You can probably think of a few times that you assumed a person's actions meant that they purposefully wanted to upset or annoy you. Maybe you thought they had a hidden agenda and you subconsciously assumed their intent. Maybe you couldn't think of any reason for their behaviour other than a negative intention.

Consider the assumptions you make each day that result from your observations of others, particularly people who act differently than you. If they value different things, you will probably see them behave in different ways. Because other peoples' intentions are invisible to you, your assumptions about their actions and words are quite likely to be inaccurate. This is due to the fact that you mistakenly assume that they see the world the way you do. You are missing important details. If you learn what's driving that person, you'll have uncovered that missing information. Be mindful of every assumption you make – which part of your assumption is the behaviour that you see, and which part is the message you give yourself based on your perceptions? Remember that the act of seeing means to "look at" an image through your eyes. Perception differs from eyesight. It is strongly influenced by your intrinsic driver. Is part of your message to yourself an assumption that is based on that filter?

When you make assumptions about why people do what they do, consider whether you're in the habit of labelling them with negative traits, like "he's so arrogant," or "she's so gullible," or "how can anyone be that intolerant?" or "I can't work with someone that rigid." When you catch yourself doing this, try to distinguish between the behaviour you see – the *what* – from the real (not assumed) driver behind it – the *why*.

Learning Nuggets

This competency is made up of the skills required to increase awareness of yourself and others.

COMPETENCY #1: ACQUIRE INSIGHT INTO SELF AND OTHERS

Remember ...

✓ Insight into yourself and others contributes to productive work relationships.

✓ You are most influential when you understand what drives you and what drives others.

✓ Passion fosters high performance – love what you do, and you'll do it well.

✓ Be mindful of your audience – think about how you see them and how they might see you.

✓ Those you work with often have different perspectives – try to see their point of view and help them see yours.

This competency focused on the *why* (your intrinsic motivation). The next competency focuses on the *how* (your intrinsic strengths). Read on for more personal leadership insights.

COMPETENCY #2: BALANCE INTRINSIC STRENGTHS

> *"The challenge of leadership is to be strong,*
> *but not rude; be kind, but not weak; be bold,*
> *but not bully; be thoughtful, but not lazy; be humble,*
> *but not timid; be proud, but not arrogant;*
> *have humor, but without folly."* —Jim Rohn

Think about how you tend to act and react in each situation in a way that inherently feels like the right thing to do. Your intrinsic strengths are your most natural behaviours. They give you energy and they contribute to your performance. They are instinctive, almost habitual ways of doing things that make you feel good about yourself. You may feel good about getting something done without delay. This could be your Drive for Achievement. Or you may value helping someone when you believe they need assistance. This could be your Drive for Affiliation. Maybe solving a complex problem that makes something work better is a rewarding experience for you. This could be your Drive for Autonomy. Whichever resonates for you, those behaviours help to build your self-worth. You probably feel like these behaviours are automatic, that you don't need to think much about them. It's true that your intrinsic strengths feel automatic because they are authentic to you and they spring from your motivation. However, in reality, you can change your behaviours and still achieve feelings of self-worth. You just need to become more mindful of the fact that your behaviour is always your choice and that you can make better choices when the situation requires a different response.

Intrinsic Strengths Are the Visible Evidence of Your Why

We can think about behaviours and intentions as an iceberg. People only see what's above the water: your behaviour (your strengths). Your intentions are invisible, hidden below the surface. The reason behind what you do or say is never obvious to others unless you choose to tell them. Most people will just assume they know why you do what you do or say what you say.

COMPETENCY #2: BALANCE INTRINSIC STRENGTHS

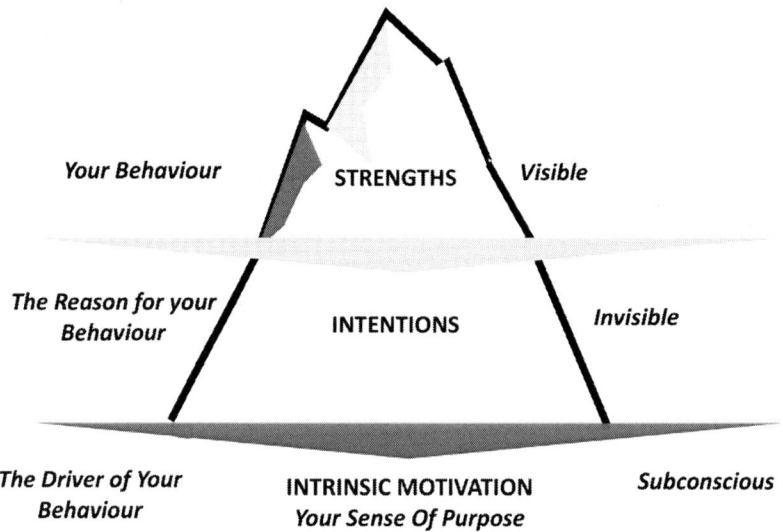

As you can probably guess, intrinsic strengths are different for different people because they are linked to each person's intrinsic driver. So, how each person perceives a strength – as good or bad – is going to differ. What becomes confusing in a work situation is the impact of these different perceptions – how the same behaviour can be perceived in a different way, depending on the perceiver.

When you work with people who share the same driver as you, you probably notice that you tend toward similar behaviours. They are likely to have the same perspective as you do regarding the right way to approach a situation. When this happens, things usually work smoothly. But there are bound to be many situations where you interact with people who have a different driver than you and who don't just see things your way. Maybe you can remember specific interactions where the outcomes didn't turn out as expected. Just because you have a predisposition to behave in a certain way, it doesn't automatically mean that things will go as expected. There are going to be situations when doing what comes naturally is not the best way for you to go. As an example, can you think of times when you have been seen as too directive, too helpful, or too practical?

Be mindful of your actions. Leadership effectiveness is all about being flexible in your approach to different situations without ever changing your why. You can still apply other strengths to serve your intention or purpose, while at the same time respecting the purpose and expectations of others. There are many ways to get the same result.

You don't want to confuse this with manipulation, of course. Manipulation is all about getting what you want at the expense of others. Everything you do should be grounded in mutual respect. Sometimes it's just good to choose a different action or response in order for someone to better understand where you're coming from. Choose your actions with an awareness of your own driver, the driver of others, and the shared goal.

Balancing Your Strengths

Within this specific leadership competency is a valuable skill: balancing your strengths to better manage your relationships in different situations. Balancing intrinsic strengths means understanding how to approach or respond to different people and different situations. When you take the time to consider how each person views your behaviour, you have the opportunity to choose a response that generates the best results with them. And when things don't turn out the way you want them to, you can reflect on why that happened and how to make better choices the next time around. It's about constantly asking yourself, why didn't my way of approaching this situation work as well as I'd hoped? How might I behave differently next time around, even if it's not what I would normally choose to do? For example, if you value getting something done without delay, what if someone perceives you as pushing to get it done at the expense of others? If you value helping someone, what if they don't want your help and perceive you to be intrusive? If solving that complex problem is rewarding to you, what if someone perceives you as slow and indecisive?

As work situations change, we often need different strengths. Be mindful of each person and situation you encounter. Each may require that you reflect on the most appropriate approach to take. You want to avoid applying too little of some behaviours or too much of others. As your career progresses, you need to be flexible in your interactions with others, even when you feel inclined to stick with old reliable ways of doing things. Your old ways won't always serve you well and, when they don't, you may need to try a different approach.

A Weakness Is Just a Figment of Perception

We can't discuss the concept of intrinsic strengths without talking about the strength-weakness paradox. This paradox is simply that every strength has the potential to be viewed as a weakness. A weakness is really just a strength perceived differently by somebody else. Every day, people are observing your behaviour and listening to your words. Without knowing it, they are expecting you to do things the way they would do them or to say things the way they would say them. If you don't, then they see a weakness.

Think of all the words that are used when someone is seen to have a weakness. Arrogant, impractical, rigid, ineffective, insensitive... the list is endless. You've probably used a few choice words yourself when describing someone you don't get along with. Any time you use a negative trait to describe someone, it's based on your perception of them doing the wrong thing. Because people have different perceptions, what you see as a weakness, someone else might see as a strength and vice versa. Remember, your judgment of someone else is through your own eyes. There are always others who will disagree with your perspective. The judgment of right or wrong is always in the eyes of the beholder. Acting in haste to get something done on time may be perceived to be too risky when it comes to quality or accuracy. Being caring or supportive in a management position may be perceived to be a sign of a weak leader. Taking time to make a well-thought-through decision may be perceived to be too slow or indecisive. Each strength will work in some situations, but not necessarily in all.

Each person brings their own expectations of you. They might believe you need to do more of one thing and less of something else. It's hard to know what each person expects unless they tell you explicitly. That's why knowing your audience is critical. If you understand another person's driver, you may be able to identify what they expect from you. If, for example, they have the Drive for Achievement, they may expect you to take swift action; if they have the Drive for Affiliation, they may expect you to stop and consider the impact on people; if they have the Drive for Autonomy; they may expect you to slow down and mitigate risks.

Can you think of a time when you failed to meet someone else's expectations? For instance, maybe you received feedback that you didn't handle a situation the right way, even though you handled it the way you normally would in those circumstances. When this happens, it helps to clarify your intent. This shifts a person's perspective from judgment to understanding. They may still not agree with your approach, but they will better understand it. And that's what matters. Similarly, when you are frustrated by another person's behaviour, take a step back and try to understand their underlying intent – their why.

Situational theories of leadership propose that your work environment determines the behaviours that would be most effective in the moment. I would add that the people involved also need to be considered. Understand the person you are interacting with and reflect on how they may be seeing you. Then adjust your words and actions to meet those expectations. That's how to get the best results in your relationships.

Organizations Focus on the *What,* not the *How* or the *Why*

In a performance management system, performance planning provides clarity around what a person is required to get done, that is, their goals and objectives. Rarely are people advised about *how* they're expected to get it done. If they go about it the wrong way, they usually find out after the fact. Never mind that they were never told what was expected of them. It was assumed they knew it through some sort of osmosis.

If your boss tells you that you are too assertive, too cautious, too caring, it's likely a sign that, in their eyes, you have overused a strength. Or, if you're told that you should have talked less and listened more at a meeting, it suggests that you were seen to have used a strength in the wrong context. Your boss may even be looking for other strengths that they personally value and believe you are underusing. The feedback might be that you need to be more confident, more cautious, more co-operative, and so on.

As you know, perceptions differ. And this is where behavioural feedback can become confusing. Perceptions of strengths and weaknesses depend on the feedback provider. When the feedback comes from a boss, then your perceived strengths and weaknesses will vary throughout your career, as you work for different managers. I worked with a food manufacturing organization that was repositioning its business in their market. Derek, the CEO, valued expediency and quick results. He had recently been appointed to this position, and the board had high expectations of his ability to improve revenues and turn the business around. Bruce, the VP of Operations, valued thoughtful process and risk management, given the need for stringency in the food manufacturing process. Bruce had a track record of high performance in his previous roles. In advance of an upcoming meeting with their investors, Derek asked Bruce for an analysis of the company's operations capabilities. He expected to receive an executive summary. Bruce, on the other hand, believed the meeting required a thorough and detailed report. Derek never communicated his expectations, and Bruce never asked for clarification. They both understood what needed to be done, but each had their own perspectives regarding what was required and different expectations regarding *how* to do it.

The Starting Point: Be Mindful

We know that situations and people determine which strengths are needed and why. It's important to think about what's required in each circumstance and for each person. Becoming mindful means developing a state of consciousness and maintaining focus on what you're doing in the moment – what you're seeing, doing, saying. We all do many things unconsciously every day. We often can't remember doing them because our minds are usually focused on something else at the same time, like a meeting we attended earlier that day or a conversation that's stuck in our heads. To be mindful means to become more consciously aware of what is happening in each and every situation. It means maintaining an awareness of our perceptions and our environment. When you practice mindfulness, you are tuned in to the other people and the situation at that moment in time. You are not focused on past behaviours, circumstances, judgments, or assumptions.

Your mind has grooves like a vinyl record. It's a system of neural pathways that form a mental map. This explains why much of what we do becomes rote behaviour. Habits are formed that become mechanical, unthinking routines. These behaviours are often derived from our repetition of thoughts and actions. When our behaviour becomes repetitive, our mindful thinking stops.

Here's an exercise often used to demonstrate how rote behaviour can be changed. Write your signature on a piece of paper. How did that feel? Comfortable, right? You didn't have to think about it, you just signed as you have done so frequently in your life. Now, switch hands and do it again. Unless you're ambidextrous, I bet you found that a lot more difficult. The result probably doesn't look as good. It required thinking about forming the letters and making them legible. It wasn't comfortable, was it? Now, consider what might happen if you lost the ability to use your dominant hand. Suddenly, you would need to write with your other hand all the time. It would feel uncomfortable at first. But over time, it would become your new normal. As they say, practice makes perfect. Rote behaviours can be changed.

Think about the situations where you've used or overused behaviours so frequently that they've become your norm, without any regard for the person or situation at hand. Just thinking about that is the first step toward mindfulness.

Think of Strengths Along a Continuum

Balancing your strengths means applying them productively. It's about being mindful in each situation of which strengths are required – understanding what will work or won't work in each situation with the specific people involved. This might mean drawing more on a strength that you rarely use or toning down a strength that you otherwise use every day.

In their article "Strengths, Strengths Overused, and Lopsided Leadership," published in the *American Psychological Association Consulting Psychology Journal: Practice and Research*, experts Robert Kaplan and Darren Overfield describe strengths according to two diametrically opposed approaches. One involves forceful behaviour, the exertion of authority, and tough decision-making. The second involves supportive behaviour, listening for input, and empowering others. Both approaches have their place. The best approach depends on the situation and the people involved. Through their research, Kaplan and Overfield discovered that most leaders tend to be lopsided. The more forceful they are, the less supportive they are. The more supportive they are, the less forceful they are. The opposite side becomes a blind spot.

When you place too much attention on the use of one strength, you can inadvertently neglect the use of a complementary strength. If you see yourself as persuasive and confident, others might see you as lacking compassion. If you see yourself as caring and supportive, others might see you as too passive or unable to take a stand. If you see yourself as logical and orderly, others might see you as lacking spontaneity.

COMPETENCY #2: BALANCE INTRINSIC STRENGTHS

The concept of the strength continuum was first introduced by Kaplan along with notable researcher Rob Kaiser. In their book *The Versatile Leader,* they explain that "effective speakers know how to modulate their voices so that the volume is neither too high nor too low.... Effective leadership requires a similar ability." It's important to modulate your strengths, so they don't appear to be too high (overused) or too low (underused). Optimal performance results from using the right strengths at the right time. For example, you can raise your level of assertiveness when persuading someone about something and lower it when collaboration is required. You can lower caution when a situation needs quick decision-making and raise it up when risk mitigation is required.

Let's think about the fact that you have many strengths from which to choose. Some are intrinsic, and some are not. You undoubtedly use some more frequently and some less frequently. Some you would choose not to use at all unless forced to. It's possible that you might overuse your intrinsic strengths because they are associated with what you value. Conversely, you may underuse strengths that are associated with what you don't value. You would avoid using those undervalued strengths even in situations where they could possibly be a better choice. Using strengths that you don't value rarely feels like the right thing to do. However, in some situations, those strengths that you don't like using could turn out to be the best strengths to use with the people involved to get you the result you need.

One of my clients, Leslie, told me about her experience in an unsuccessful job interview with the senior partner of a professional services consulting firm. Her intrinsic strengths associated with her Drive for Affiliation created a less than favourable impression on the senior partner. As she reflected back on that interview, it was apparent that, from his perspective, she had failed to demonstrate the strengths he was looking for. In hindsight, she agreed that instead of appearing humble, friendly, and deferential, she would have fared better toning down those strengths and focusing on appearing assertive, confident, and persuasive.

Another client, Keith, the CEO of a multidivisional manufacturing company, told me about a similar learning experience. Keith's preferred management style was engaging and collaborative. He preferred to defer decisions to his team, and his meetings sometimes ended up being prime examples of all talk, no action. At the end of one particularly long meeting, one of his executives made the comment, "it's great to be a team player, but every once in a while, the team needs a quarterback." Keith hadn't realized the level of frustration his team experienced when a situation warranted swift action and he didn't take any. Although his team valued his flexible approach, there were times when being too inclusive and open to other points of view prevented him from drawing timely closure on key business decisions. Keith needed to learn how to strike the right balance. As a remedy, Keith ensured his team knew it was safe to give him feedback on his meeting management, and he became mindful of those times the team required a more directive approach.

How to Use Strengths Productively

To measure whether you are using your strengths productively, focus on the impact these strengths have on you (did you achieve your intended result?) and on others (did the other person respond in an expected way?). In other words, do the results meet your expectations and your desired outcomes? And do they also meet the expectations and desired outcomes of the other person or persons? If so, then your strengths were engaged productively. If not, you are probably not getting optimum results in your relationships.

I had a client named Jim, who's a perfect example of someone who entered a role where his strengths became unproductive. Jim was a successful manager who was appointed to a temporary leadership role in a different division. In the first couple of weeks, Jim didn't read the work culture of his new environment. He valued getting things done in a timely way, and he saw the opportunity to make immediate changes and introduce some new initiatives. Unfortunately, Jim's new team culture valued thoughtful regard for established procedures and due diligence. Within a couple of weeks, Jim's new boss sent him back to his previous position, recommending that a coach be hired to fix his leadership problem. Jim was confused. He was doing what he did best – the very actions that had gotten him nominated for the role in the first place. They were the ones that got him the best results.

Unfortunately, what Jim had failed to notice was that those strengths weren't valued so highly in his new environment. Instead of being respected, he was viewed as having failed. This was a humbling experience but a valuable one. Jim's failure had nothing to do with his capability. Unknowingly, he hadn't taken the time to understand his new boss's expectations. Nor had he understood how he needed to behave differ-

COMPETENCY #2: BALANCE INTRINSIC STRENGTHS

ently to achieve the same objectives. Perhaps a more methodical and collaborative approach would have worked better. Jim's story is a good example of the strength-weakness paradox. Strengths and weaknesses are always a matter of perception. Whether a behaviour is viewed as a strength or a weakness depends on the situation and the perceivers.

Reflect on the strengths you often use. Perhaps you overuse them because they're your go-to behaviours. These strengths can be perceived as weaknesses. If you value getting things done, you may naturally want to be somewhat forceful and directive in your approach. One observer might see a strength: you are confident and efficient. Another observer might see a weakness: you are too pushy and domineering. Now, look at the strengths you use much less frequently, or maybe never. These are the ones that you underuse. If you tend to be directive, that same observer who saw you as pushy is probably expecting to see more collaborative behaviour, so they view your lack of that strength as a weakness.

UNDERUSED / Too Little   PRODUCTIVE / Just Right   OVERUSED / Too Much

Think about how others perceive you in terms of your potential strengths and weaknesses. If you use your preferred strengths all the time, in every situation, or to an extreme, what are the risks in your relationships? The following charts show how strengths can be perceived differently. Remember, these are only examples of behaviours that are intended to be productive because they are most closely aligned with an internal driver and a person's underlying intent. As you can see, every strength can be productive (centre column), and every strength has the potential to be perceived as underused (left column) or overused (right column), depending on the situation and the people involved.

Part Two: Personal Leadership Competencies

STRENGTHS RELATED TO THE DRIVE FOR ACHIEVEMENT

When Underused *Perceived* As...	When Productive *Perceived* As...	When Overused *Perceived* As...
Insecure	Confident	Arrogant
Cowardly	Daring	Reckless
Apathetic	Ambitious	Pushy
Ineffective	Persuasive	Bullish
Weak	Directive	Overbearing
Passive	Enterprising	Aggressive
Unambitious	Competitive	Combative
Unassuming	Proud	Conceited
Timid	Bold	Brash

STRENGTHS RELATED TO THE DRIVE FOR AFFILIATION

When Underused *Perceived* As ...	When Productive *Perceived* As...	When Overused *Perceived* As ...
Suspicious	Trusting	Naïve
Callous	Supportive	Subservient
Unreliable	Faithful	Servile
Unrealistic	Idealistic	Impractical
Uncaring	Helpful	Stifling
Arrogant	Modest	Self-Effacing
Apathetic	Devoted	Doting
Unfeeling	Compassionate	Soft
Inconsiderate	Polite	Deferential

COMPETENCY #2: BALANCE INTRINSIC STRENGTHS

STRENGTHS RELATED TO THE DRIVE FOR AUTONOMY

When Underused *Perceived* as…	When Productive *Perceived* as…	When Overused *Perceived* as…
Irrational	Analytical	Analysis Paralysis
Careless	Thorough	Compulsive
Unrealistic	Practical	Unimaginative
Impulsive	Cautious	Apprehensive
Chaotic	Orderly	Rigid
Wasteful	Economical	Stingy
Brash	Reserved	Shy
Unjust	Fair	Insensitive
Insecure	Self-Reliant	Aloof

As you review the strengths above, you might recognize that all these strengths can serve you at one time or another. Strengths that are typically associated with each driver can function as a simple how-to guide. You can identify the strengths you need in each situation in order to get better results. Remember that your intrinsic strengths have the potential to be perceived as overused, and your non-preferred strengths may be perceived as underused. Be mindful of how your strengths are perceived both through your eyes and through the eyes of others.

Sometimes we learn by observing others. Look closely at the people you most admire. What strengths do you see them use? How do they behave in different situations? Where do they use their strengths most productively? Would you like to become more comfortable using those strengths yourself? If so, practice these new behaviours in situations where you want to be seen as doing your best. Become the person you aspire to be.

Part Two: Personal Leadership Competencies

Learning Nuggets

This competency is made up of the skills required to act and interact productively with others.

Remember...

- ✓ Your intrinsic strengths come from your drive for self-worth.
- ✓ Each of your strengths has the potential to be viewed as a weakness – it depends on the perceiver.
- ✓ In every interaction, your actions have an impact on others – consider how others might see you.
- ✓ Behaviour is a choice – if you aren't getting the results you want in your relationships, change your approach.
- ✓ Relationships stay healthy when you choose the right strength, in the right situation, at the right intensity.

COMPETENCY #3: COMMUNICATE WITH INFLUENCE

> *"Many relationship problems are rooted in a communication breakdown. These can be as simple as not really hearing what the other person is saying, because we get caught up in our own fixed perspectives."* —Sumesh Nair

Influencing is one of the most challenging and valuable aspects of leadership. When you work with others, you need people to get your message and understand your intent. Communicating with influence is critical for personal leadership because you need to be able to bring people along to your way of thinking without the use of direct power. Perception plays an important role when it comes to influencing others. Often, people don't understand what you are trying to say because what they hear or see is filtered through their perceptions. We may think we have been understood or that we understand someone else, but we are only filling in the gaps of information based on our own interpretations – what we believe to be true.

Communicating with influence requires two separate but equally important things: clarity of expression and active listening. Clearly expressing your ideas helps the other person understand you, and active listening allows you to understand them, including their perspectives.

As I've said before, people often confuse influencing with manipulation. Manipulation is based on your interests alone, but influencing is always based on addressing the other person's interests as well as yours. The art of influence is simply taking the time to know your audience and to use that knowledge in your interactions with them.

If you've ever been successful in convincing someone to change their perspective, think about why that worked. If another person has been successful in getting you to see things their way, what did they say to you that made the difference?

Robert Cialdini, author of the book *Influence: The Psychology of Persuasion*, notes two important concepts. The first is that we are more easily influenced by people who value what we value. The second is that people are more likely to commit to something they regard as important or meaningful. The key to successful influencing is remembering that when someone doesn't understand why something is important, from their perspective, it's not likely that they'll want to commit. Before you approach someone, even if the matter seems unimportant, stop, look, and listen.

STOP: Be mindful of what you say or how you say it before you speak. Focus on your intention and your goal. What do you expect from this interaction? What do you want the other person to hear and understand? Be honest and direct. Create trust.

LOOK: To understand how someone is responding, concentrate on all visual cues. Look at their facial expressions. You may get a sense of how they are feeling. Do they appear angry, confused, uninterested? Do they make eye contact with you when speaking? Do they seem relaxed or tense? All these cues help to understand their personal reactions to your message.

LISTEN: Influencing also includes being open to hearing another person's point of view. When you are able to see things through another person's eyes, you have a greater probability of gaining their agreement.

Take the time to put yourself in their shoes. Consider how things might look from their perspective. What might they like about it? What might they resent? Watch their reactions and listen to what they say. Show that you appreciate their perspective.

Influential Communication is More than Words and Actions

Think back to a time when you listened to a speaker who just read the words on a page, where there was no passion, no energy – just a sharing of information and data. Not very inspiring, right? Now think of a speaker who held your attention and encouraged you to listen more intently. I bet their impact wasn't just related to the words they were saying. Speakers that inspire and influence have a way of building our confidence and trust in them. We believe that what they're saying has value. That's what I call *effective relating*. They connect with their audience in some way and their message resonates. Something sparks our personal interest.

When it comes to influence, you need to consider why your audience would choose to buy into what you believe is important. Remember, your audience can be an individual person, or a group – a collection of individuals with different interests and perceptions. To influence, you need to respect the perspectives of everyone in your audience.

To influence those around you, consider the two most important factors: *what* you're talking about and *who* you're talking to. Ask yourself if your message is relevant and why. Will it be seen as relevant to others? If yes, why? You need to consider the potential that others won't see the purpose or benefit of what you're proposing. Your message could be viewed as irrelevant or even unacceptable. Before engaging with others, consider if that's a possibility and why that might be.

The ABCs of Influence

You can use an easy ABC structure to frame your communication approach:

A) Acknowledge Individual Interests – Understand and focus on what each person deems important. In other words, ask yourself, "what's in it for them and why would they be interested in listening further to what I have to say?"

B) Build on Shared Interests – Look for common ground. Think not only about your interests but the other person's interests as well. Then look at those you both share and help the other person see them too.

C) Connect to Communicate – Connect with them by showing an interest in their perspective. Actively listen for the meaning behind the words you hear and take note of what you see. Does the other person look confused, annoyed, interested, or uninterested? Refrain from criticism. Suspend judgment and demonstrate respect for their perspective.

Part Two: Personal Leadership Competencies

Shift your Focus from Debate to Dialogue

Part of your ability to connect with your audience includes a conscious shift from *telling someone something* to a *conversational exchange of views and perspectives*. This is important to remember, particularly if you believe that the logic of something is enough to get someone to see your point of view. If you do, you will more often be met with resistance, not agreement. A conversational exchange happens when you shift your approach from debate to dialogue.

A dialogue requires both hearing and listening. They are different terms. Hearing the words is not the same as understanding the meaning behind them. In psychology, the term active listening is referred to as *listening with the third ear*. This concept, first introduced by psychoanalyst Theodor Reik, refers to the practice of listening for deeper layers of meaning behind the words. It's listening to the person's intent, not simply hearing their words.

Debate	Dialogue
Focus on own ideas	Open to new ideas
Unwilling to shift position	Willing to shift position
Wait to speak	Actively listen
"Prove" orientation	"Explore" orientation
Focus on winning	Focus on understanding
Make statements	Ask questions
Knowledge as a "weapon"	Knowledge as a "gift"
Avoid risks	Take risks
Low interpersonal trust	High interpersonal trust
Focus on facts	Focus on facts and feelings
Intolerant of differences	Embrace differences
Focus on "what I know"	Focus on "what I can learn"

COMPETENCY #3: COMMUNICATE WITH INFLUENCE

Define Your Sphere of Influence

Now that we've talked about how you can more effectively influence others, think about the work relationships in your sphere of influence that would benefit most from applying these concepts. Influence requires understanding the people in these relationships. The odds of being most effective at influencing and engaging them increase when you appreciate their sense of purpose. How do you perceive each of these people – what adjectives would you use? Refer to the words used to describe productive strengths in Competency #2. What words would you choose for each person? What do you believe is most important to each of them? Now, consider the quality of these relationships. Is there someone with whom you would like to communicate influentially? If so, review some of the ideas you've discovered.

Complete the following image to define your sphere of influence. Which are your most important relationships? What are the risks if any of these relationships are not productive?

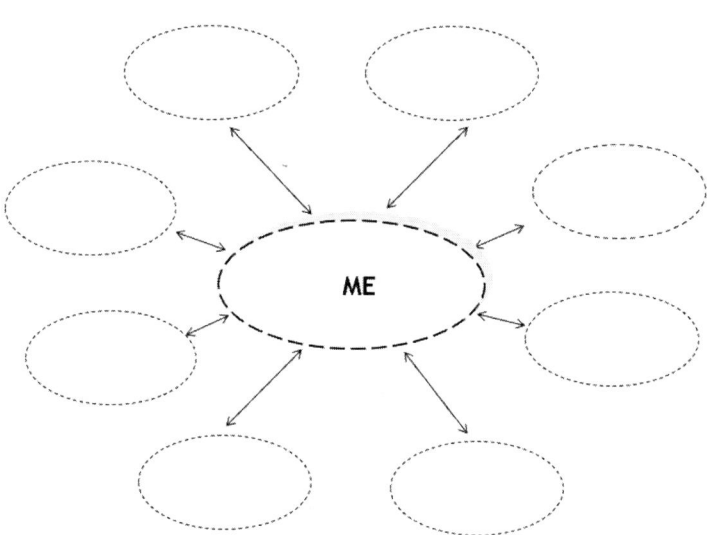

Part Two: Personal Leadership Competencies

Don't Forget to Manage Up

Sometimes when we think of our sphere of influence, we focus only on our colleagues because we most often interact with them. However, don't forget that one of your most important relationships is the one you have with your manager. The phrase *manage up* refers to the process of mindfully working with your manager for mutual benefit. Managing up is another way of saying *learn how to influence your boss*.

You may think you don't have significant influence over this relationship, but you do. As with all relationships, a productive one requires observing how they act and react in different situations and understanding what drives them.

Reflect back to a time when you needed to persuade your manager to view a situation from your perspective. What was the situation? What was the result? What did you do that worked well or didn't work well? Looking back, could you have done something differently and produced a better result?

I had a great manager early in my career. Everything I saw this person do represented what I wanted to see in a boss. During my career, I also worked with quite a few managers that I viewed as ineffective. Of course, they weren't really ineffective. That's just how I saw them. Obviously, not everyone saw them the same way. Labelling those bosses as ineffective was saying that they didn't meet my expectations of what a good boss should be. Those relationships were not ideal. Looking back, I can see that I was accountable for the outcomes of my relationships. I had the power to make those relationships more productive.

We've talked about how our intrinsic driver influences how we judge people and what we expect of them. It's clear that I judged previous managers as ineffective because, from my perspective, they didn't value what I valued. They didn't reward me in ways that were meaningful to me.

Research from the Wharton School of business found that many direct reports don't spend enough time managing upward, as they don't realize how important it is. Often, they focus on other priorities and accept the fact that they just don't get along with their boss. Personal differences in behavioural styles can create low trust and a lack of mutual respect. These are contributing factors to non-productive "boss/subordinate" relationships.

COMPETENCY #3: COMMUNICATE WITH INFLUENCE

Stay alert to cues that are helpful for understanding what drives your boss – what you believe they're most concerned about. A proactive approach here goes a long way toward creating a relationship that respects individual differences. You need to be able to see the world through their eyes. It's critical to understand their perspective and then look for common ground. Pay attention to what you perceive their interests to be, as well as their underused or overused strengths. Be aware of their blind spots and potential conflict generators so that you can respond appropriately.

While You're At It... Clarify Expectations

You are in a partnership with your boss. In any partnership, it's crucial that both parties understand what each one expects from the other. This is an important and often overlooked part of the job. You both have perceptions of how each of you is expected to behave in your respective roles. As we now know, perceptions differ. So, these differences in relational expectations inevitably lead to conflict if they're not clarified. Are you aware of, and do you understand, the expectations your team leader has of you? Clarify expectations regularly in your relationship. Continually ask for feedback and seek agreement:

- Discuss *how* you are expected to fulfill your objectives.

- Share your understanding of the expectations you believe your manager has of you and your role.

- Let your manager know what expectations you have of them. Say, "for me to be effective, this is what I need from you."

- Identify the interests and needs that are essential to you.

- Acknowledge your manager's interests and needs.

- Clarify assumptions. It is too easy to fall into the trap of agreeing to a deadline of "some time next week" or "ASAP" or "as soon as you get to it." These sorts of minor agreements lead to major misunderstandings.

Part Two: Personal Leadership Competencies

- When your expectations do not align with those of your manager, ask for clarification, and listen for understanding, with a view to reaching agreement.

Learning Nuggets

This competency is made up of the skills required to be influential in your work relationships.

Remember...

✓ Communicating with influence means taking the time to know your audience.

✓ Influence involves both expressing your viewpoint and listening to the viewpoints of others.

✓ The better you get to know people, the more likely you are to influence them productively.

✓ Take the time to put yourself in someone else's shoes – understand what they deem important.

✓ Ask yourself how and why someone might view things differently, then try to see things from their perspective.

People who learn how to apply this competency are particularly adept at preventing, managing, and resolving conflict. And that's Competency #4.

COMPETENCY #4 PREVENT, MANAGE, AND RESOLVE CONFLICT

> *"In some ways, we will always be different. In other ways, we will always be the same. There is always room to disagree and blame, just as there is always room to take a new perspective and empathize. Understanding is a choice."* —Vironika Tugaleva

Imagine working on a project team. Midway into the project, you are called to a meeting where the team is informed of a unilateral decision to change the agreed mandate. You're upset with the leader's message. You begin to challenge the leader in an argumentative way. You notice that a few people have visibly become silent and withdrawn. Others nod and smile, seeming to be agreeable, but they appear anxious and uncomfortable. Are they not bothered by this news? You're confused. Why aren't they speaking up?

We can all be fooled by the behaviours we see in others. Some reactions that look like conflict aren't, and some that don't look like conflict, are. Someone could be in conflict and you could have absolutely no idea. Not all conflict is visible. Most of us think it looks like anger, but that's not always the case. Unfortunately, if someone is upset and doesn't show it, it's not likely that you'll get to a resolution. You can't resolve a conflict that you don't even know exists.

You benefit from gaining insight into different conflict responses. If you understand what another person is experiencing, you automatically see things from a different angle – not just yours. You can become adept at preventing conflict before it happens and resolving it when it does.

Relationship Acuity plays a major role in every aspect of conflict, from prevention through to resolution. You cannot prevent, manage, and resolve conflict without awareness and understanding – awareness that we all view conflict in different ways, and understanding that we differ regarding *what* conflicts means to us, *why* we go into conflict, and *how* we are likely to respond. This starts with understanding the two main types of conflict:

Part Two: Personal Leadership Competencies

- The first type of conflict is *intrapersonal* and relates to conflict within yourself. It's an internal experience related to your values, feelings, actions, and emotions. You experience this type of conflict when you're required to do something that conflicts with what you believe is the right thing to do. In this regard, it's important to have insight into your own intrinsic driver. It helps you understand why you're conflicted. You can also apply this insight to understanding the reasons that others may experience this type of conflict.

- The second type of conflict is *interpersonal* and relates to conflict between you and others. This conflict may occur when you work with people who see things differently than you do. They might say and do things that annoy you. You wouldn't work with them, given the choice. Just remember that they may, in return, perceive you the same way. When it comes to interpersonal conflict, perception is an important variable. If you can't see what other people care about, you must sharpen your lens to better understand where they're coming from.

Let's look further into the meaning of conflict. While the word often conjures up images of two people shouting at each other, that's not the only way that conflict can manifest itself. In a dictionary, you'll see several synonyms for the word. Some seem slightly negative, such as disagreement, dispute, or quarrel, and some quite strongly negative, like war, battle, and combat. Others suggest something more positive such as engagement, difference, or drive. Just like these synonyms, people differ in what they think conflict means and what it looks like. What does conflict look like to you? Consider the words, feelings, metaphors, or responses that you personally associate with it. Your perception of conflict can trigger certain emotions in you. These perceptions reflect your own internal values and experiences.

To fully understand the meaning of conflict, you need to identify the reasons that conflict occurs in the first place. As I've said before, most people try to do what they believe is the right thing. Conflict occurs when your right seems wrong to someone else, and vice versa. Each of you sees it differently, and that triggers an emotional response. Think back to a time when someone ignored you or dismissed you when you

COMPETENCY #4: PREVENT, MANAGE, AND RESOLVE CONFLICT

were talking about something you felt strongly about. How did that make you feel?

Not everyone responds in the same way when they experience conflict. If the usual image of conflict is arguing and fighting, don't be fooled into believing someone is experiencing conflict when you see them loudly arguing their point of view. If they seem to be enjoying the argument, they probably aren't in conflict; they're just forcefully expressing their point of view and they probably do enjoy it. Conflict, by contrast, is something people *don't* enjoy. We don't enjoy feeling stressed, frustrated, or angry. Conflict starts with a difference of perspectives in which each person takes an *either/or* position. Either we do it the *right* way, a.k.a. my way, or the *wrong* way, a.k.a. your way. Interactions then become unpleasant. Negative feelings emerge. The discussion becomes personal and emotional. As you can imagine, if the root cause of the conflict isn't addressed, a resolution is unlikely. Instead, it becomes a never-ending cycle of misperceptions, negative feelings, and dysfunctional interactions. Left unresolved, a conflict is bound to escalate. Small differences can become major battles that no one ever wins.

Building Relationship Acuity includes learning how to prevent conflict from happening, manage it when it does, and resolve it to ensure your relationships remain productive. *Preventing* conflict requires an understanding that people value different things. *Managing* conflict requires knowing that people respond differently in conflict. *Resolving* conflict requires learning how to solve problems that are rooted in each person's intrinsic driver.

Preventing Conflict: Understanding Our Different Intrinsic Drivers

There's a difference between conflict and opposition. Opposition is based on differences of opinion. It's rational and productive. It's often referred to as healthy debate, and it's something that organizations should encourage because out of opposition comes new thinking and more creative ideas. Conflict, on the other hand, is something you want to prevent. It's based on the differences between what people value. It's emotional, unproductive, and personal. *While managing opposition requires an understanding of the issues, managing conflict requires an understanding of the people.*

Part Two: Personal Leadership Competencies

Preventing conflict starts by understanding how you and others might look at things differently because you value different things. When two or more people are driven by different things, there is always the potential for conflict. If something is important enough to you, and others ignore or devalue it, it will trigger an emotional response. Review the following interests that often relate to each driver. They represent what a person might deem important. Which ones resonate most with you? When working with others, observe their words and actions. Over time, you can get a sense of which of these might resonate most for them.

People with a Drive for Achievement are interested in *results*, and they focus on:

- Productivity
- Outcomes
- Growth
- Goal attainment
- Winning
- Competing to win
- Task accomplishment
- Profitability

People with a Drive for Affiliation are interested in *relationships*, and they focus on:

- Service
- People
- Helping
- Supporting
- Kindness
- Altruism
- Compassion
- Loyalty and allegiance

COMPETENCY #4: PREVENT, MANAGE, AND RESOLVE CONFLICT

People with a Drive for Autonomy are interested in *reason*, and they focus on:

- Reliability
- Quality
- Logic
- Thoughtful analysis
- Mastery
- Competence
- Proficiency
- Self Sufficiency

When you are aware of another person's driver, you have a head start in understanding why they might experience conflict. Something has threatened what they value. I call these threats conflict catalysts. Catalysts are charged issues that generate emotion because they stem from a person's sense of purpose. They can sidetrack you, making your emotional brain take over the rational side and often making you literally stop listening. They might make you act impulsively and do things you wouldn't normally do. In these highly charged moments, it can take some time for your emotions to settle down. And although these situations are disturbing to you, they may not arouse the same response in others.

Here are some typical catalysts related to each driver. Check off the ones that resonate with you.

Catalysts Related to the Drive for Achievement

Because you value *results*, you may experience conflict when...

- ☐ There appears to be no goal or action toward goals
- ☐ Results get stalled
- ☐ No one is leading; decisions aren't being made in a timely way
- ☐ You see time being wasted on unimportant or trivial matters
- ☐ Everyone is talking; there's no action
- ☐ Your efforts to take charge, when needed, are rejected

Part Two: Personal Leadership Competencies

Catalysts Related to the Drive for Affiliation
Because you value *relationships*, you may experience conflict when...

- ☐ People appear rude and arrogant
- ☐ There is no recognition for your efforts
- ☐ You observe frequent confrontational behaviour and ongoing conflict
- ☐ There is poor communication or no communication at all
- ☐ You see hidden agendas and trust is low
- ☐ Your efforts to help, when needed, are rejected

Catalysts Related to the Drive for Autonomy
Because you value *reason*, you may experience conflict when...

- ☐ There appears to be no structure or organization around you
- ☐ You see people acting without thinking, doing it quickly rather than doing it right
- ☐ Decisions are made without logic
- ☐ People don't give you the personal space you require
- ☐ Approximations are accepted at the expense of accuracy
- ☐ Your efforts to do things correctly, when needed, are rejected

When your emotions take over, it's a sign that you have entered conflict. When this happens, you need the requisite skills to manage the conflict and to move toward a resolution.

Managing Conflict: Understanding the Conflict Response

"Things would be better between us if only ~~you~~ *I* would..."

When you change the way you look at things, you can change how you respond. For example, remove the word *you* from the following sentence and replace it with the word *I*. Do you feel the shift in accountability?

Remember that you are always accountable for your outcomes in each conflict situation you experience.

COMPETENCY #4: PREVENT, MANAGE, AND RESOLVE CONFLICT

Your conflict response may be based on your belief that it's the best way to manage your conflicts. However, I'm sure you can think of times when your response didn't lead to a desirable outcome. If that happens often, it's important to understand why.

Here's a simple exercise to consider your conflict response. Reflect on two or more recent interpersonal conflicts. For each situation, first think about why you were in conflict (your catalyst), then try to remember what you did (your response). When you reacted, did you:

A. Fight?
B. Smooth things over by giving in?
C. Avoid interacting?
D. Solve the problem?

As you might guess, A, B, and C are less productive responses. They are built-in reactions to threatening situations – they usually fail to resolve the conflict and sometimes lead to heightened conflict. We have circuits hardwired into our brains that lead us to react reflexively when faced with threats – this is called the fight-or-flight response. When faced with a threat, we experience a surge of adrenaline to assist us with either fighting or fleeing. Our heart rate and blood pressure increases, and our senses become hyper-alert.

Daniel Goleman, author of the best-selling book *Emotional Intelligence*, refers to this stress response as the "amygdala hijack." Your amygdala is the part of your limbic system that processes your emotions. This hijack occurs when your brain senses a threat. The thinking part of your brain shuts down and the information you perceive is routed directly to your amygdala to prepare you to fight or flee. The bad news is that this hijack affects your ability, in the moment, to manage the situation objectively and constructively.

Do you tend to visibly vent your frustrations? Do you delay dealing with important issues? Or do you give in grudgingly without voicing your concerns? If your answer is yes to any of those questions, your response in conflict is probably often ineffective. The good news is that you can change your response by changing how you look at the situation. With the right to be heard comes the responsibility to listen and be open to influence. You must be mindful of the people involved.

When you express your emotions in constructive ways and engage in productive dialogue, people see you as effective. And that's how you

Part Two: Personal Leadership Competencies

can make conflict work for you. For example, imagine that you are struggling to accomplish an objective in a tight time frame, and someone asks you to drop what you're doing to provide them with some information they need. You think it's unreasonable that they'd expect you to meet their request when you're so busy. A non-constructive response would be, "You know I'm already snowed under with my own work. Why would you ask me for anything right now?" This response puts the other person into a defensive position and can easily lead to an argument over whose needs are more critical. Alternatively, a more constructive response might be, "I've got a lot on my plate right now. Tell me more about your problem so I can better understand your urgency." A response like that could prevent potential conflict and lead to a negotiated solution.

Recognize the Conflict Response in Yourself and Others

You've stepped into conflict with both feet. The first thing you need to know is that managing conflict requires a combination of responses, depending on the situation and the people. If the other person is not in conflict, focus on what they care about and be sure to connect the potential consequences of an unresolved situation with the risk to what *they* care about. If the other person is in conflict, remember that they are in an emotionally charged state. They may need and want different things and respond in different ways than you do.

Understanding conflict reactions starts by looking at your own. There may be a time when you need to be assertive in order to express your needs. At other times, you may need to be responsive so that you build trust, or logical if you need to focus on facts. Which approach you use depends on what the other person needs in the moment. Do they need you to speak up because they want to know where you stand? Do they need you to actively listen to them and be responsive to their concerns? Do they want you to remain objective and separate the problem from the person? What does the other person need and expect from you? Asking them what they need might be a good starting point.

According to Marshall Sashkin, author of the *Conflict Style Inventory*, the most common styles are fighting and withdrawing, since those represent the common reflexive fight-or-flight responses. Smoothing over and problem-solving are the least-used styles.

Elias Porter's research on conflict went further to understand that each of us has our own unique and predictable response that is rooted in the motivation that drives us in conflict. This motivation is different than our intrinsic motivation when things are going well. You may sense a shift in motivation as you enter conflict. As a result, behaviours change in response to this shift. If you do not experience a shift in your motivation early in the conflict, you may experience it later when the conflict escalates. Porter also discovered that there are three basic responses when we enter conflict, based on what we want at the time. We either want to speak, we want to think, or we want to listen.

When you become aware of how you usually respond as you enter conflict, you become more aware of what you want in each situation. You also become more aware of what you want and expect from others. In turn, you can observe how others respond in conflict and begin to understand what they may want and expect from you.

The four main styles of behavioural responses are what I call the Four Cs:

Confrontational Style

- **How it's perceived:** A confrontational style is often perceived as fighting or arguing. You speak directly to the other person and voice your position forcefully. You get straight to the point. You speak more than you listen. You send the message that your own concerns are more important than the other person's.

- **What you want:** You want to be heard. You want the other person to see your point of view and agree with your perspective on the issue. You want to deal with the situation without delay. You need the other person to engage immediately and to resolve the issue as quickly as possible.

- **What you expect:** You expect the other person to take you seriously and listen to what you have to say. You don't expect them to ignore you, walk away, or delay the discussion in any way, even if there is a risk of conflict escalation. You do not expect them to make light of the issue or ask you to "calm down."

Part Two: Personal Leadership Competencies

Contemplative Style

- **How it's perceived**: A contemplative style is often perceived as avoiding the issue, stepping back, or becoming disengaged. You take the time to analyze the situation and examine all the facts about why the conflict occurred. After the requisite time for analysis, you are then willing to rationally discuss the situation with the person or persons involved.

- **What you want**: You want adequate time to think about the situation. You want to analyze and process all the relevant facts. You want to carefully examine the reasons that the conflict has occurred, including how you might have contributed to the situation yourself.

- **What you expect**: You expect a full, rational response from the other person. You expect them to calmly discuss the facts about the conflict and look at ways to resolve it. You don't want the other person to approach you in an emotional or aggressive way.

Conciliatory Style

- **How it's perceived:** A conciliatory style is often perceived as deferential, non-assertive, or compliant. You approach others respectfully, ask questions, and listen carefully for their concerns. You might bend to the will of the other person and put their needs and concerns ahead of your own to keep the peace.

- **What you want:** You want to understand where the other person is coming from. You want to meet their needs, even if it means putting your own needs aside. You want a solution that preserves the relationship.

- **What you expect:** Because you focus on listening to their concerns and understanding their perspective, you expect the same in return. You expect them to respond in a calm and respectful manner.

Convergent Style

- **How it's perceived:** A convergent style is often perceived as objective, open-minded, and goal-focused. You focus on the problem, not the person. You state the issue clearly and give your perspective about why it's important. You ask how the other person sees the situation. You listen to understand the other person's viewpoint in an objective, non-emotional way.

- **What you want:** You want the other person to understand your perspective. You want to clarify your assumptions and understand their point of view. You want a mutually agreeable solution that maintains a productive relationship.

- **What you expect:** You expect both parties to be rational, to focus on each person's interests, and to be open to hearing different perspectives. You expect each person to be honest and willing to suggest different options for a resolution.

Which described style do you believe you use? Reflect on the styles you have observed in others. Which tends to irritate you? Which ones do you value and why? From your perspective, what is the value of each style? What are the blind spots of each style?

What Happens When Your Approach Doesn't Get You the Results You Expect?

Pushing for a quick resolution risks being perceived as too aggressive or threatening. Spending too much time processing information risks being perceived as trying to avoid conflict or having no interest in solving the problem. Giving in to avoid further conflict risks being perceived as being too passive or non-assertive.

Although you may have a preferred conflict response, you'll benefit from using a different approach when it's warranted. A confrontational response works best if you're dealing with a person that values a more forceful argument. A contemplative response works best when you feel the need to defer interacting with the person involved. You might choose a conciliatory response when you feel your energy is best saved for a more important issue. A convergent response is ideal when both parties agree to focus on solving the problem and generating solutions.

Part Two: Personal Leadership Competencies

The best conflict response is the one that applies the skill of influence, especially when you value the relationship. Step back, examine the situation objectively, sharpen your perception of the other person and adjust your response accordingly. When you do this, you are managing conflict effectively and taking a step toward a resolution. It would be very naïve, of course, to believe that every conflict gets resolved this way. There will be situations when you recognize that it's time to exit a discussion or perhaps even end a relationship. But when the issue is important, it's worth the effort to work toward a productive outcome.

Empathy Always Counts

Empathy is an important ingredient in conflict management. It involves perceiving the emotional state of another person, using a style of listening in which you put aside your self-interests and work to genuinely understand how the other person feels. The focus is on the other person, not you.

Empathic listening helps you control your emotions by replacing your anger or frustration with imagining what it would be like to walk in the other person's shoes. It gives you a better understanding of their perception of the situation and their response to it. To listen with empathy, create the goal of understanding instead of replying. We often empathize with people who are most like us, but when we most need to empathize is when we're managing conflicts with people who have different perspectives.

Think about a particularly challenging work relationship you have, one that you need to improve. Try to identify why you perceive the person the way you do. What misperceptions may have contributed to those challenges? What are some of the things the person does or says that are your conflict catalysts? What could be their underlying intent or motivation?

Conversely, what are some of the things you do or say that they might describe as a conflict catalyst for them? Think about how beneficial it would be if the other person understood your intent.

Resolving Conflict: Applying Purpose-Based Problem-Solving

Because conflict catalysts are rooted in what we care about, conflict resolution requires an understanding of why the conflict occurred in the first place. That's why the key to resolving conflict is applying what is commonly known as interest-based problem-solving.

There's truth in the saying *two heads are always better than one*, and it applies nicely to a conflict resolution process. You want to employ a problem-solving process that deals with the problem, not the person – keeping emotions under control and considering the facts, not the people and their personalities. In interest-based problem-solving, both sides are involved in creating a mutually agreeable solution.

Just as importantly, the focus in conflict resolution must be on interests, not positions. That's why I refer to this approach as purpose-based, because a person's interests are always rooted in their sense of purpose. When it comes to interpersonal conflict, a successful outcome must address expectations that are rooted in each person's drive for self-worth. *What's in it for me?* becomes *What's in it for both of us?*

Purpose-based problem-solving starts by considering the three intrinsic drivers – achievement, affiliation, and autonomy. Remember that each driver represents its own unique purpose. There's a direct connection between our intrinsic driver and what we value and pay attention to. Spend some time determining which intrinsic driver best applies to each person in the conflict.

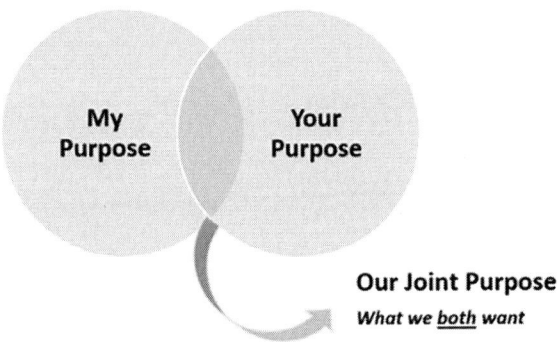

Armed with this information, you are now in a better position to create the conditions that will lead to an effective conflict resolution. Now you can consciously move from a message framework (trying to prove you are right) to a learning framework (trying to understand the other person's interests). The whole process is about addressing what each person deems important, recognizing your respective conflict catalysts, and jointly creating a productive outcome.

One way that differences create conflict is by creating win/lose situations. Human nature has us believe that one person must win and the other must lose. We use energy to defend our positions. And when rank and status are involved, the person with more power, more often than not, is the one who wins. Most disputes involve a conflict of positions. A *position* is the outcome that each person believes is the right solution, and *the only one*. Your *interests*, on the other hand, represent your intrinsic needs. While a position is typically rigid, interests can be met in a variety of ways. When you look behind opposing positions to see purposeful interests, you can find alternatives that have the potential to meet both your interests and theirs.

Be aware that if you're always trying to prove that you're right, you'll close the door to further dialogue. Without dialogue, there can be no new insights that help to dispel incorrect assumptions of intent. All your energy goes toward justifying your beliefs rather than working toward a resolution.

If, instead, you explore what each person in the conflict values, you can shift the focus to the question, "how can we address this issue while recognizing what we each need and want?" This is the best way to arrive at a solution that is acceptable to both sides.

A Simple Process for Purpose-Based Problem-Solving

The first step in purpose-based problem-solving is to clarify perceptions to discover the root cause of the issue. Seek to understand the reason that the conflict exists in the first place.

Next, use your skill of influential communication – listen to learn. Find out what's important to them – their *why*. Share what's important to you, too.

Identify who is upset and why. What are the catalysts that spurred the conflict in the first place?

Then, connect each person's purpose to the underlying issue. What does each person want as a potential solution?

Finally, identify a shared purpose that honours the values of both sides.

COMPETENCY #4: PREVENT, MANAGE, AND RESOLVE CONFLICT

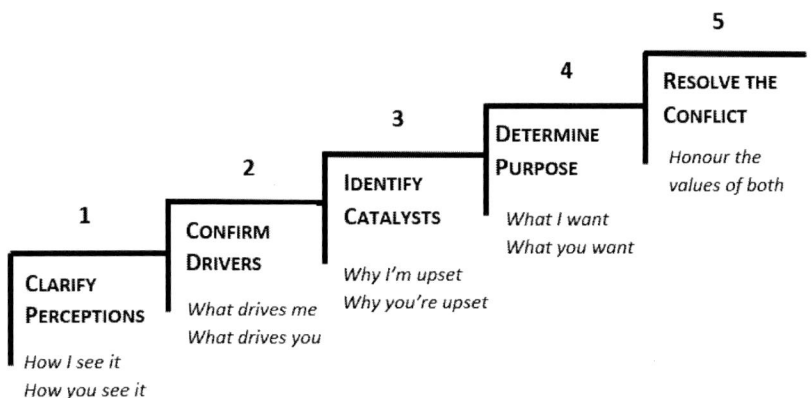

The most important ingredient in conflict resolution is fostering a dialogue. From a conflict perspective, dialogue literally means using words to move people through an interaction that uncovers new meaning. We've already talked about the importance of transitioning from debate to dialogue. Dialogue allows for an exchange of ideas. It demonstrates your desire to further understand the issue and the other person's point of view. Ask questions, and actively listen. With each question, let them see that it comes from a sense of curiosity, not a position of certainty. Your questions should imply, "help me understand why this is important..." Make sure to share your assumptions regarding the conflict and remain open to hearing theirs.

Learning Nuggets

This competency is made up of the skills required to prevent, manage, and resolve interpersonal conflicts.

Remember...

- ✓ People go into conflict for different reasons; they have different conflict catalysts that are linked to their drive for self-worth.

- ✓ When in conflict, people react in different ways – some reactions don't look like conflict to others. Some people appear argumentative, some appear compliant, and some appear quiet.

- ✓ Be mindful of the impact of your perceptions when in conflict. You only see people's behaviour, not the reasons for it.

Part Two: Personal Leadership Competencies

✓ Pay attention to your assumptions and potential misjudgments when you view the behaviours of others.

Conflict is inevitable. As much as you can become skilled at preventing it, there will be times when you feel unable to do anything but react emotionally. Strong emotions result in a stress response. Learning how to manage that response is an important leadership skill. And that's Competency #5.

COMPETENCY #5: BUILD RESILIENCE

> *"The difference between successful people and others is how long they spend feeling sorry for themselves."*
> —Barbara Corcoran

My father was a professional violinist. For over twenty-five years, he was the director of music with one of Canada's most prestigious hotels. Every night, his trio of violin, cello, and piano provided music for the diners in the hotel's main dining room. Even though I was quite young at the time, I remember the day he was given his two-weeks notice. The hotel was under new management and the formal dining room was to be permanently closed. There was no severance payout. He had no pension and no other means to earn money. And making a living in music was difficult at that time. But my father turned the challenge into an opportunity: he started a new career as a piano tuner, building on his contacts in the music community. I can't help but reflect now on how my father dealt with such a crisis in his life. Throughout my own career, I have coached many people who have lost their jobs. Many react with anger or fear. Some struggle to move on. In contrast, my father changed his profession in mid-life, with optimism and enthusiasm. By the time he retired, he had built an established business with over 5,000 clients.

People say it's not what happens to us but how we deal with it that makes the difference. Simply put, resilience is not only a leadership competency; it's a life competency. Resiliency refers to how we each perceive the challenges we face every day and our response to them. Being resilient requires looking at things from a perspective of growth, not defeat.

We hear stories of people who suffer setbacks in their lives but for whom those challenges seem to fuel their drive for success. How is it that they are able to succeed? These are people who, in the face of adversity, become even stronger and continue to thrive. What is it that carries these people through their tough times? It's the capacity for resilience. It's an enviable quality for people who struggle with challenging situations. Salvatore Maddi, founder of the Hardiness Institute, refers to resilience as a form of hardiness. When people are resilient, they seem to find meaning in terrible times. They have the uncanny ability to see the positive and to make the proverbial lemonade out of lemons.

There's a misunderstanding that resilience somehow means being strong and fearless. This definition creates a potential problem because when you believe it's wrong to be fearful, you develop the fear of fear itself. Fear, however, is a normal human reaction. Everyone feels it. People just react to it in different ways. Some people take on things they're afraid of, while others try to avoid them, focusing on the reasons something *can't* be done. Which group are you in and how's that working for you?

Staying in Your Comfort Zone All the Time Is a Recipe for Stagnation

Humans are designed to be challenged. Challenges lead to accomplishments, and pressure motivates us to do our best. Even failures have the potential to lead to personal growth. When it comes to stress, there's an optimal zone between over- and under-stimulation. We need stimulation to inspire positive action, but not so much that it paralyzes us. Learning to be resilient is about learning how to respond to challenging situations in a way that balances our stimulation zone. This optimal zone is where we develop new insights and have the capacity to exert our maximum discretionary effort.

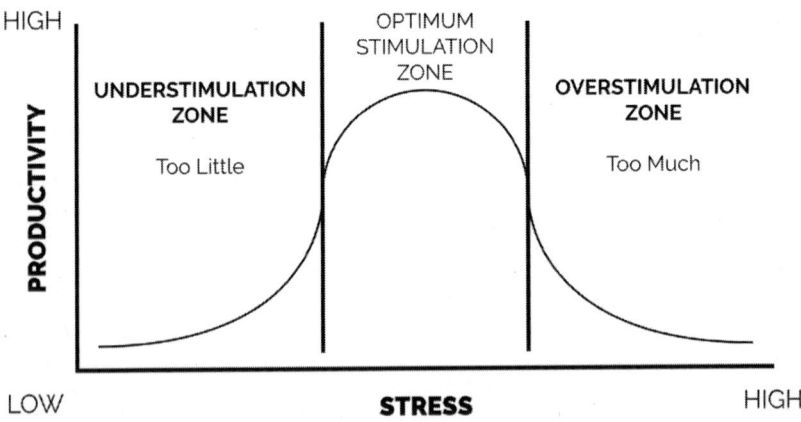

Much has been written about the foundational skills of resilience. In the context of Relationship Acuity, resilience is related to the ability to *sharpen your perception of the situations you encounter.* This includes being mindful of where you sit on the stress curve, shifting how you look at stressful situations, generating energy and engagement, and seeking meaning in your work and your work relationships.

Resilience Is Influenced by the Power of Pull Motivation

In any challenging situation, you are either pushed or pulled into action. Tension is created by either a push away from something or a pull toward something.

Push motivation is tension from an external change that gives us energy to move from something undesirable, while pull motivation is different and more positive. When you're being pulled to do something, energy to move comes from within. It's something you personally want.

It has often been said that a person with big dreams is more powerful than one with all the facts. Many of us label our dreams as fantasies and put them on the back burner, but some people's dreams pull so strongly that they devote incredible amounts of energy toward reaching them. That's how they respond to creative tension. The way to understand that tension is to imagine you're holding an elastic band tightly between two hands. Now pull one hand away. The tension in the elastic grows. To release the tension, you can either hold on and force the hand that moved away to move back again, or you can allow the other hand to follow the first one. If the leading hand is forced to move back, nothing changes. That's how many of us live our lives: by resisting change. But some people release the tension by moving toward what's pulling them forward. If you want positive change, you need to create a vision of what you want and allow that pull motivation to move you toward your goal.

The *I Have a Dream Foundation* has helped over 18,000 students get to and through college. The foundation's website describes its historical beginning in 1981. Eugene Lang, its founder, was asked to talk to students at the East Harlem elementary school that he had attended fifty years earlier. Before his speech, the school principal told Lang that three-quarters of the school's students would probably never finish high school. Hearing this, Lang adjusted his speech. He said to the students that if they stayed in school, he would pay each of their college tuitions. Of the original 61 students, more than 90% earned their high-school diplomas and 60% pursued higher education. Lang had given them hope and a chance to dream.

People's visions or dreams are not often taken seriously – by parents, by teachers, by guidance counsellors, and by bosses. Under the guise of representing reality and experience, these people say things like, "You need to set your sights on something that's within your reach, something more realistic." But sometimes, we're better off when we aren't realistic. When we think about limits, we're the ones creating them. The older we get, the more realistic we become. We think we know what can and can't be done, what we are and are not capable of... what's possible and what isn't. Then we proceed to fire hose our dreams with a dose of "who am I kidding?"

The only reality that serves you is the one that says you are the person in charge of your own life. It's not what happens to you that matters; it's what you do about it. Success comes from putting your thoughts into action instead of passively waiting for things to change. Before entering any new situation, give yourself a positive mental picture. Focus on a vision of what you want to have happen and where you want to go. See yourself accomplishing it. That will go a long way toward developing a can-do attitude that puts control back inside you, where it belongs.

Sometimes You Need to Step Back and Look with Fresh Eyes

Resilience is not a trait that people just have or don't have. It's a habit you can build by allowing yourself to look for hidden opportunities. It's about making a conscious decision to change your habits. Habits represent the way you have always done things. Building resilience means breaking some of those habits and developing a new and different perspective. Remember the exercise where you signed your name with your non-dominant hand? It felt uncomfortable. But, with practice, it could become more comfortable. The same holds true for changing patterns of beliefs and behaviours. It will feel uncomfortable at first, but with time and practice, you can find success!

Albert Ellis, the creator of Rational Emotive Behaviour Therapy (REBT), discovered that people's irrational beliefs often lead to self-defeating habits. His work is grounded in the idea that people want to succeed, but their irrational thoughts often get in the way. Ellis developed an approach that I've found to be especially important in helping people manage challenging situations. It involves shifting our way of looking at things. The following is an adaptation of his approach.

COMPETENCY #5: BUILD RESILIENCE

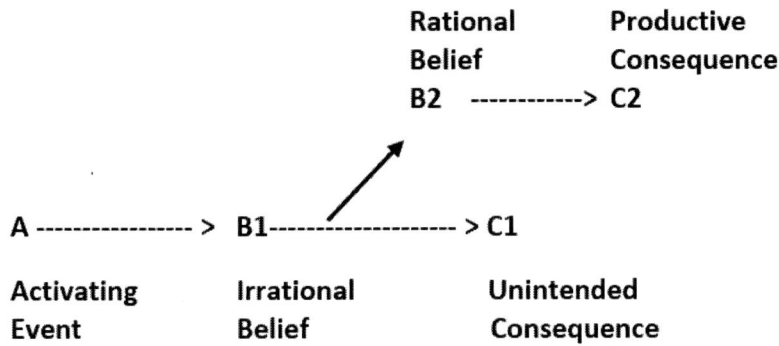

It starts with an activating event (A). The event causes an internal reaction that creates an irrational belief (B1). As a result of this belief, there is an unintended, usually undesirable consequence (C1). You often don't realize that this consequence is the result of your irrational belief, not the initiating event itself. Let's say, for example, that you've been asked to do a major presentation to a group of senior leaders in your organization. You begin to worry about it. What if you make mistakes and people think you're ineffective? That irrational belief begins to take hold. You start thinking you're going to fail. You develop an unconscious list of *must* statements for yourself, which lead you to feel incompetent and inadequate: I *must* do this perfectly, or I'm going to be seen as a failure; I *must* give a flawless presentation, or they're going to see me as incompetent; I *must* not make any mistakes, or my career is bound to be ruined. Then, when you give the presentation, all your energy is focused on this irrational belief rather than on just delivering your message competently (the way you are perfectly capable of doing!). It easily becomes your self-fulfilling prophecy.

New beliefs lead to different behaviours. In turn, new behaviours lead to better outcomes. Consider the same event (A) and with a new *rational* belief (B2) that could result in a more productive consequence (C2). Replace the *must* statements with more realistic ones. They can be as simple as: "I can't control how others see me; I can only do my best," "If I make mistakes, I'm going to learn from them," or "My presentation probably won't be perfect, but I'm going to make sure that I have all the facts to support my data." Notice the change in focus. It shifts from fear of the outcome to trying to do your best. Your energy goes toward the presentation, not the fear.

When Perceptions Change, Outcomes Change

Throughout your career, it is inevitable that you will encounter roadblocks and setbacks. How you perceive these experiences determines how you handle these stressful situations. This is where the power of perception applies. How do you see each situation you encounter? Where do you focus your energy?

There's a well-known story about a psychology professor conducting a stress-management class. (I can't seem to identify where it came from, but the moral is a good one.) The professor, as the story goes, raises a glass of water in front of her students, who expect to hear the typical glass-half-full/half-empty lecture. Instead, she asks them to guess the weight of the glass of water. After listening to a few replies, she says that the absolute weight of the glass doesn't matter. If she held it for a minute or two, it would feel fairly light. If she held it for an hour, it would likely feel heavier, and her arm might begin to ache. If she held it for an entire day, the pain and strain might force her to drop the glass to the floor. The weight of the glass remains the same – only the length of time changes. The longer you hold it, the heavier it feels.

Stresses in life are similar to this glass of water. Think about them for a while, but don't carry them around all day. They'll become increasingly heavy and you'll be incapable of doing anything until you drop them. As with the glass of water, put it down for a while. Lighten the stress – then look at things with a different perspective.

What's Change Got to Do With Resilience?

Change is constant. It's the only thing we can be sure of. Building resilience requires shifting your perception of the changes you encounter every day – the changes that take you out of your comfort zone. Every change you experience brings the potential for experiencing losses and gains. I've seen first-hand how people are affected by the stress of imposed changes in the workplace. They see only losses, while gains may as well be invisible. Resilience is the ability to see those gains.

Someone once said that the only people that welcome change are babies. Nobody else, it seems, welcomes it with open arms. No matter how positive the change, our human tendency is to resist it because we want to hang on to the familiar. We stick with what we know, we play it safe, and we gravitate to the familiar. After all, we've been conditioned

COMPETENCY #5: BUILD RESILIENCE

as children to believe in continuity and predictability. We fear that change will only make matters worse. We even resist change when things are *not* going well. If we're dissatisfied with our work, we stick it out. Better to stay with the devil we know.

Many changes are those that we don't want or would not have chosen, given the option. When it's not our choice, we see change as beyond our control. It happens *to* us, and we feel unwilling and ill-prepared. Imposed change can be challenging. You may experience fears and irrational thoughts. People often report experiencing fear of the unknown, a loss of personal control, a lack of clarity of purpose, and feelings of incompetence. On top of that, the internal question "WIIFM?" is always in the background, determining how you respond.

Think of how often you've heard people say, "It'll never work," "It's not practical," "Things are fine the way they are," "We've never tried anything like that before, why start now?" or "That's not the way we do things around here." You may even have made some of those comments yourself, at one time or another. If you don't like change, it probably has a lot to do with a preference to stay in your comfort zone. I have worked with many coaching clients who preferred to stay in a job they didn't enjoy for security reasons, a sense of comfort, a fear of failure, or a hesitation in facing the unknown.

It's often easier to stay where you are rather than face an uncertain future. You think the pain of leaving will be far worse than the pain of staying, so why not stay? Better to just wait for the crisis to happen, right? But when it does, the pain of staying becomes greater, and that's when you might finally jump ship – staying is no longer tolerable. Unfortunately, when you hit a crisis point, you risk making the jump without a thoughtful plan about what you need or where you need to go.

Change might occur as a result of something you initiated yourself, such as choosing to move to a new job. It can also be something you didn't anticipate that was initiated by others. Either way, it involves a journey from your present state to a future state.

Change always starts with something ending. It brings a sense of loss. Facing change means letting go of something familiar in order to move toward something new. This journey involves navigating an in-between zone – it's your road to getting there. In this zone, you've left the present, known state, but you haven't yet arrived at the new unknown. What makes this in-between zone so disorienting is that, frequently, you don't yet understand the future state well enough to know exactly where you're going or how to get there.

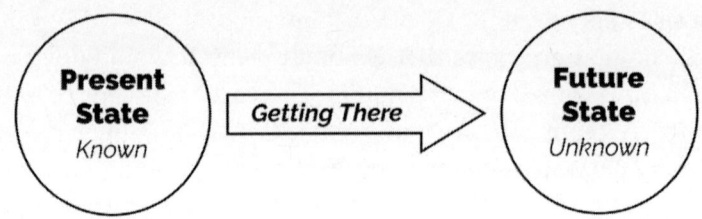

The Two Sides of Change

The definition of crisis often includes two opposing concepts – danger and opportunity. Change has the potential to bring both. Sometimes what appears to be a threat is a hidden opportunity, seen only when we view the situation in a different way.

The real danger in any change process is the potential loss of the possible opportunities it brings. Consider the potential dangers and opportunities that exist in a change you are currently experiencing. Notice the shift in focus when you move to the words on the right.

PERCEIVED DANGERS

- Loss of purpose
- Loss of self-confidence
- Not knowing the future
- Lacking required skills
- Being stuck
- Lacking clarity

HIDDEN OPPORTUNITES

- Re-establishing purpose
- Renewed confidence, building new strengths
- Perceiving new challenges
- Learning new skills
- Becoming re-charged
- Creating a clear picture

When You Perceive Danger, You Need a Sense of Personal Control

In their book *Resilience at Work: How to Succeed No Matter What Life Throws at You*, Salvatore Maddi and Deborah Khoshaba talk about the importance of gaining a sense of personal control. This sense of control empowers you to feel you have some influence over the challenges you are experiencing. Psychologists call this your *locus of control*.

Your locus of control reflects how you perceive a stressful situation. It's how you react and your beliefs around whether you can or cannot make a difference. You either believe you have control over your life

COMPETENCY #5: BUILD RESILIENCE

and are responsible for managing it, or you believe you are controlled by outside forces, with no control.

When you have an *internal* locus of control, you believe positive or negative outcomes are the consequence of your own beliefs and actions. You are confident in your ability to do something about your situation. You expect outcomes based on your own personal effort or behaviour and can plan the steps and strategies to achieve them. You believe in taking calculated risks, seeking opportunities, and persevering in the face of challenges.

On the other hand, if you have an *external* locus of control, you feel you are controlled by outside forces. You have a sense of learned helplessness. Common expressions include "It's their fault," "It's impossible," "There's no point, I can't do it," "That's the way it's always been," "I'm just not lucky," "I never had a chance," and "If only..." When you have an external locus of control, you are consumed by wishful thinking or belief in the power of luck or fate, instead of accountability. This becomes counterproductive because it deprives you of initiative, energy, and optimism.

When a situation at work becomes challenging, don't blame your colleagues, your boss, or your organization. That does nothing but make you feel helpless and hopeless. Blame may alleviate your responsibility for the situations you face, but it makes you powerless.

Focus on What You Can Control, Not on What You Can't

In terms of the changes that you are currently facing, make a list of the things you believe you *cannot* control.

CANNOT CONTROL	CAN CONTROL

Review the list of *cannot control* items and determine if, in fact, you could have some influence over any of them. If so, move them to the *can control* side.

To regain a sense of control, focus your energy on what is controllable, and minimize your worrying about what is not. As the following image demonstrates, when you focus on what you feel you *can't* control, you just end up with endless worry. Focus on what you *can* control, and you have the potential to see new opportunities. All your energy is channelled toward constructive problem-solving.

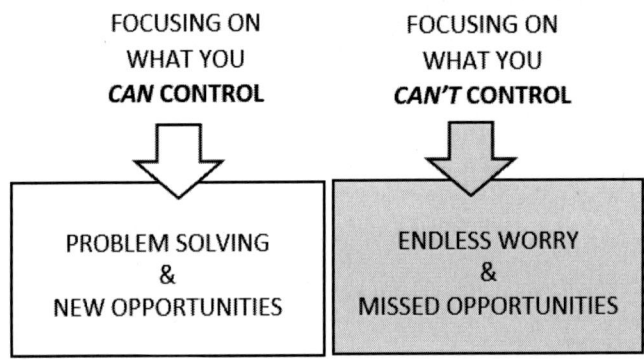

Your Organization Is Changing: Welcome to Transition

Change is an event. It is situational and external to you. Something stops; something starts. It's usually quick, results-driven, and impersonal. Transition, on the other hand, is internal. It is slower, loss-based, and personal. It is a gradual adaptation to external change. The timing of each person's transition process is defined by where they *are*, not where they *should be*.

You have likely experienced moving to a new house. The change is the actual move itself, from the planning through to the packing, transporting of belongings, and unpacking at the new place. Your transition experience, on the other hand, is your internal emotional response to that change. Think about the actual amount of time required for the physical move. It's usually one or two days. Now consider how long it takes to feel comfortable and familiar in your new surroundings, get to know the neighbourhood, develop new routines, and make new friends. That takes much longer. And moving around the corner is different than

COMPETENCY #5: BUILD RESILIENCE

moving to a new country. The bigger the change, the longer you may stay in transition.

Even if everyone experienced the same changes, we all have different internal reactions to those changes. Each person is focused on how they feel about the change.

There are many current change models. The model I prefer derives its inspiration from the work of Elisabeth Kübler-Ross, author of the internationally best-selling book, *On Death and Dying*. Cynthia Scott and Dennis Jaffe first presented their change model in their article "Survive and Thrive in Times of Change," published in the *Training & Development Journal*.

The image below shows an adapted version of Scott and Jaffe's model, which involves four distinct psychological stages of transition. We all move through these four stages at different speeds.

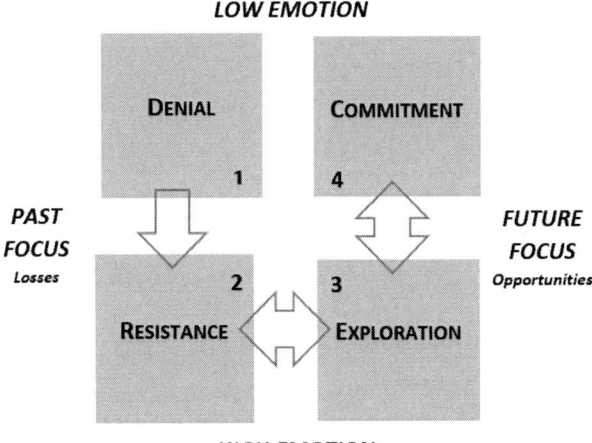

The Scott and Jaffe Change Model
Adapted from C. Scott & D. Jaffe, 1988

To understand this model in terms of resilience, it is best to look at what each side represents. On the left side, the focus is on the past. When you are in Denial and Resistance (stages 1 and 2), you only see losses. On the right side, the focus is on the future. When you're in Exploration and Commitment (stages 3 and 4), you see opportunities. The greater your degree of resilience, the more quickly you will likely move from the left (past focus) to the right (future focus).

121

Part Two: Personal Leadership Competencies

As you transition through change, you move through the four stages in sequential order. However, as the arrows indicate, once you come out of Denial, you are likely to oscillate back and forth between the three remaining stages as a change process evolves. You might at one point feel you've moved into Exploration, but then something happens that takes you right back to Resistance. And, because change is constant, even if you arrive in Commitment, you may not stay there long.

In Stage 1 (Denial), you aren't paying much attention to the impending change. That's a natural defense mechanism. It is easier to ignore what's going on around you than to face it. You may not even recognize that you're in this stage or even be aware of your internal reactions. The reality has not sunk in, so you avoid thinking about it and stay focused on the status quo.

Eventually, a feeling of discomfort comes along that leads you to Stage 2 (Resistance). This is when you experience the impact personally. Something has threatened your comfort zone. Your focus shifts from outside to your internal emotional state. Feelings of fear, anger, sadness, or anxiety surface as you try to hang on to what is familiar. In this stage, you may begin to distrust those in authority. Your performance could suffer. It's natural to want things to remain as they are, to hold onto what is comfortable. Even when the change brings an element of excitement, there's anxiety about an uncertain future. Resistance is normal because you're being asked to give up something familiar. Learning how to deal with this stage of transition plays a large part in building the skill of resilience.

In Stage 3 (Exploration), your focus shifts to the future. You begin to take positive action, learn new ways of doing things, and decide how to move forward with confidence. Instead of working against the change, you begin to ask yourself how to make it work. You remain focused on yourself, with a more positive outlook that gives you some much-needed energy.

In Stage 4 (Commitment), you're proactive. You make decisions and take actions to master what's needed. These experiences build resilience. What you've learned along the way serves you well. Even though you have, figuratively speaking, arrived, the reality is that you still need to prepare for the next change that's coming your way.

If you're feeling stressed or angry about a change, understand that it's normal. Be aware that you focus first on what you perceive you are giving up. You see losses before gains. It's okay to legitimize your losses. They are real for you. Most of us can only handle so much change at once. Set priorities for yourself and only do those things that are necessary right now. Share your ideas and concerns with people you trust.

How each person perceives a change is often different from the way others see it. People are always at different levels of readiness and acceptance. With this in mind, don't judge others without first understanding where they are and what they might be most concerned about.

Where Are You?

If you could use one word to describe how you feel about all the changes going on around you, what would that word be? It could be any word: anxious, excited, angry, sad, frustrated, energized. The word should reflect your current emotion. The word you choose helps to identify what state you might be in. Does it reflect indifference, negative emotions, positive excitement, calm?

Now, consider how you are responding. Typical reactions provide yet another clue.

Typical Reactions in Each Stage

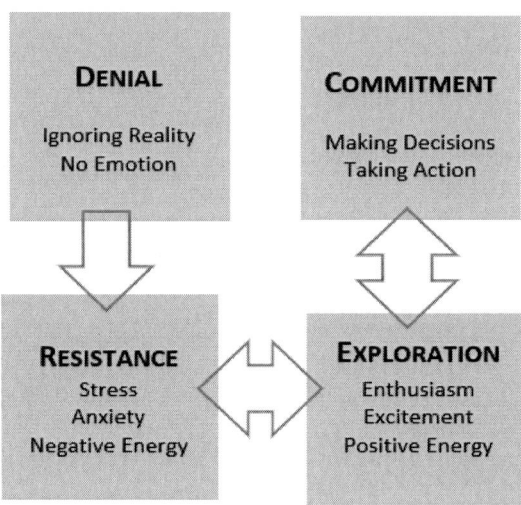

Based on that word you initially chose, and your current behaviour, you may be able to identify where you are in your transition process.

Part Two: Personal Leadership Competencies

Strategies for Building and Sustaining Resilience in Transition

Now that you understand the stages of transition and have identified where you may be in the change process, focus on ways to build your resilience. Each stage requires a different strategy, as summarized in the chart below. In Denial, you may need more information to separate the rumour mill from reality. If you're in Resistance, seek emotional and practical support from people you trust. In Exploration, create a positive vision of what you want to happen, clarify your goals, and be open to alternatives. If you've reached Commitment, reflect on what you've learned and continue to look to the future.

TRANSITION STAGE	YOUR STRATEGY
STAGE 1: DENIAL	GENERATE UNDERSTANDING – *Make sense of what is happening and why*
STAGE 2: RESISTANCE	SEEK SUPPORT *Both emotional and practical*
STAGE 3: EXPLORATION	TAKE PERSONAL CONTROL *Make sure you are in control of the impact of the change on you*
STAGE 4: COMMITMENT	DEFINE A SENSE OF PURPOSE *Generate personal meaning around your goals and actions*

Learning Nuggets

This competency is made up of the skills required to build resilience in today's complex and high-change world of work.

Remember ...

- ✓ Embrace your sense of purpose and visualize what's possible.
- ✓ Seek the goals that give meaning to your work.
- ✓ Change *what if* to *if... then*. Focus on what you *can* do, not what you can't.
- ✓ Imagine achieving what you want and expect success.

COMPETENCY #5: BUILD RESILIENCE

- ✓ Seeing is believing – create a vision for where you plan to be in two years.
- ✓ Clarify your vision – make it real. Where are you? What are you doing? How do you feel?
- ✓ Create your plan to get to where you want to be.

This completes the five foundational Personal Leadership competencies. You are now ready to learn about the second set of competencies that focus on building the competence to lead others.

TEAM LEADERSHIP COMPETENCIES

Achieve Results Through Others

"Forget praise. Forget punishment. Forget cash. Make their jobs more interesting instead."
—Frederick Herzberg

Organizational Leadership
- 12. Transform Culture
- 11. Inspire Purpose, Vision & Values
- Generate Corporate Energy

Team Leadership
- 10. Lead the People Side of Change
- 9. Mediate Conflicts
- 8. Build Cohesive Teams
- 7. Coach for Acuity
- 6. Facilitate Performance Potential
- Achieve Results Through Others

Personal Leadership
- 5. Build Resilience
- 4. Prevent, Manage & Resolve Conflict
- 3. Communicate with Influence
- 2. Balance Intrinsic Strengths
- 1. Acquire Insight into Self and Others
- Develop Personal & Interpersonal Effectiveness

Part Two: Team Leadership Competencies

Team Leaders Achieve Results Through Others

"Leaders' passion, energy, and focus beget passion, energy, and focus in their workers. Watch a great conductor or football coach in action and you will see what I mean. The members of the orchestra or the team are not dutiful but inspired." —Warren Bennis

It is difficult to lead others if you don't first understand how to lead yourself. That is why I presented personal and interpersonal competencies as the foundation of leadership. Now we're moving to the competencies that form the next set of building blocks – the ones that enhance your ability to achieve results through others.

Perception plays a significant role in team leadership. You must now see things through the eyes of each of your direct reports – your associates. Motivation also plays a significant role. At the heart of every team is a sense of purpose that binds people together. A team's sense of purpose, when aligned with each team member's personal purpose, ignites the energy needed to facilitate optimum performance.

When your goal is to maximize the potential of your team, remember the basic premise: each team member's intrinsic driver influences their perceptions – of themselves, their colleagues, the situations they face, and you, their leader. In turn, their perceptions drive the behaviours they choose when working with each other.

It's All About Inspiring Others

Team leadership means being able to ignite energy in others. When you recognize each person's intrinsic driver, when you facilitate honest and candid dialogue, and when you provide meaningful performance feedback, you are well on your way to becoming an inspiring team leader.

An inspired person believes their work is meaningful. What each person sees as meaningful relates to their own personal sense of purpose. Early in my consulting practice, I would occasionally offer free advice when asked. In return, I often received personal notes of thanks, which I found extremely rewarding. I took a lot of pride in those notes. I shared one meaningful card with a colleague, and he immediately

Achieve Results Through Others

turned it upside down, asking, "Where's the money?" To that colleague, payment was far more meaningful than any thank-you card.

Understanding the factors that affect motivation, expectations, and performance will serve you well in your role as a team leader. When people are inspired, they want to achieve their best. Know that the most significant rewards are those that satisfy each person's purpose. The best thing you can do is help each associate better understand themselves, what they value, and how they can achieve outcomes that feed their self-worth.

Each of your associates is unique and their individuality needs to be understood. Make it your job to understand what drives each of your team members. Consider how to spark their energy. What do they value? Be open to appreciating their unique perspectives. That may sound like a lot of work, especially when you have your own goals to achieve, but know that when you put in the effort to understand your associates at a deeper level, you will create less work for yourself in the long run.

Remember, team leadership depends on relationships that are built on transparency and trust. You create these relationships by seeking to understand those who work for you, what drives their behaviour, and what gives them a sense of purpose in their work.

How Do Your Associates See You?

At this point, you've reviewed the five foundational Personal Leadership competencies. If you demonstrate those competencies, your associates are bound to understand that you are someone who is authentic and accountable for your behaviour. They see you as someone who is self-aware, an active listener, open to influence, respectful, collaborative, and resilient. Now, to master team leadership, it's time to add this next set of building blocks: the five Team Leadership competencies.

The Starting Gate

To begin, ask yourself honestly how often you demonstrate the following team leadership behaviours. Think about your experiences and the behaviours you demonstrate on a day-to-day basis. Put a check mark in the box that you believe is appropriate for each behaviour.

Part Two: Team Leadership Competencies

How Often Do I...?	Almost Never	On Occasion	Almost Always
1. Foster productive relationships on the team			
2. Create an environment that values individuality			
3. Strengthen individual feelings of self-worth			
4. Listen openly to varied perspectives			
5. Make it safe to challenge the status quo			
6. Encourage open dialogue and constructive debate			
7. Provide opportunities to learn and develop potential			
8. Provide meaningful feedback and recognition			
9. Create a climate of trust and mutual respect			
10. Encourage reflection, insight, and resilience			

If most of your check marks fall under *almost always*, you see yourself as an effective team leader who leads a highly productive and engaged group of people.

Next, consider how your team members see you. Put yourself in their shoes. Do you think they see you the way you see yourself? Ask each of your associates to fill in the following chart. When you compare the two, are there any differences? If so, why do you think that is?

Achieve Results Through Others

How Often Does My Team Leader...?	Almost Never	On Occasion	Almost Always
1. Foster productive relationships on the team			
2. Create an environment that values individuality			
3. Strengthen individual feelings of self-worth			
4. Listen openly to varied perspectives			
5. Make it safe to challenge the status quo			
6. Encourage open dialogue and constructive debate			
7. Provide opportunities to learn and develop potential			
8. Provide meaningful feedback and recognition			
9. Create a climate of trust and mutual respect			
10. Encourage reflection, insight, and resilience			

The behaviours listed in the above two charts represent the skills in the five Team Leadership competencies. Let's look at each of these competencies in more detail.

COMPETENCY #6: FACILITATE PERFORMANCE POTENTIAL

> *"Loyalty is earned by the way you treat [people].*
> *People don't leave jobs; they leave managers they*
> *don't want to work for."* —Tom Rath

Healthy relationships play a direct role in achieving performance potential. They count just as much as the structure, policy, and processes of management. Productive relationships generate commitment. And without commitment, people won't give their best. Committed people do whatever it takes to get the job done. Now, think about what you do that encourages your associates to *want to* perform at their best.

Warren Bennis is well known for having quoted that many organizations are "over-managed and under-led." For years, performance management systems have been designed to help managers make sure their employees do what they are required to do. Forms and scripts are provided for annual reviews that document whether employees have accomplished their objectives, met their deadlines, and achieved expected levels of performance. No one can argue that performance management isn't a necessary process, but there's more to inspiring performance potential than filling in forms.

The link between employee satisfaction and productivity has long been established. Research has found that satisfied workers are far more productive than unsatisfied ones. Engaged and committed associates are worth more than their weight in gold. They go the extra mile. Don't assume your associates are committed just because they're getting paid a fair wage. Commitment isn't for sale. It must be earned. How you treat your employees counts. Without the drive and energy of an engaged and committed group of associates, your team won't reach its performance potential.

Relationship Acuity and Performance Potential

Facilitating performance potential means engaging in conversations that support the performance management process. Performance management usually includes establishing performance objectives and assessing the achievement of those objectives at year-end. In between, managers engage with their employees to ensure they stay on track to deliver expected results. You enhance this process when you build productive relationships with each of your associates, clarify the purpose of their role, and acknowledge their contributions in meaningful ways.

The Role Perception Plays

We've talked a lot about the fact that people differ in what they believe is important. So it's logical to assume that they also differ in what they think it means to be a leader. I can think of many times that I was asked to design leadership training programs when the definition of a leader hadn't even been clearly established by the organization. To me, this is a flawed approach. How can you assess people on their leadership capability when everyone has a different definition of leadership? To prove this point, ask a few of your associates to define what being a leader means to them, then note the different responses. They reflect each person's perception, and their judgments and expectations of a leader.

Just as each associate is judging you based on what they value, you, in turn, judge each person based on what you value. Today's knowledge-based jobs do not readily lend themselves to objective criteria. More often than not, subjective opinions are involved. These opinions are shaped by your individual perceptions as the team leader. Be sure your observations and judgments aren't clouded by a biased perspective, or *perception attribution error*, which means making inferences about someone based on one's subjective interpretation, without any objective data to support it. A simple example would be the tendency to look at an associate's substandard work and infer that the person was incompetent. To assume that incompetence was the reason for this issue is probably inaccurate – under-performance could result from any number of factors. It's best to gain insight into the true reason for the issue before jumping to any conclusion. If you catch yourself depending on your own subjective interpretation of a person, remember: it's a *performance* evaluation, not a *person* evaluation. Your opinion about who is a good performer or a bad performer is just that: an opinion.

Part Two: Team Leadership Competencies

Be Mindful of Imperceptible Expectations

Even when you're clear with yourself that you're evaluating someone's performance rather than them as a person, there are other traps to be aware of. Before you assess how they've performed against your expectations, ensure you've made your expectations abundantly clear. Sometimes you believe people are on the same page, seeing something the same way you see it when they're really not. Imagine you're frustrated by one of your associates who clearly isn't showing a sense of urgency in getting an important job done. You call them on it. "Why didn't you get it done? It was a priority." In response, your associate points to their inbox and reminds you that everything has been labelled a priority. Which priority did you want your associate to focus on? Your poorly communicated expectations led to confusion.

Differing role expectations are rarely discussed. I'm not talking about clarifying *what* needs to get done – that's a given. I'm referring to *how* your associates are expected to get it done. If your associates don't know your expectations, how are they going to do what you expect of them? How can they be expected to improve? Are they expected to be directive, collaborative, prudent? Should they work independently or seek the input of others? Should they step up and take charge, or step back and allow others to make decisions? Clarify *how* you expect them to go about getting their job done.

While communicating expectations is critical, don't forget to also find out the expectations your associates have of you. You need to frequently ask the question, "How am I doing?" Sometimes the answers can surprise you.

The Motivation Factor

Each of us unconsciously judges every situation according to its perceived value. When it comes to motivating your team, you need to look beyond the value of compensation alone. If an associate sees no purpose in their work, they very likely won't give all their energy to it. Someone who values working independently is not going to enjoy a role that requires constant team interaction. A person who cares about people and relationships will become de-motivated if forced to deliver poor service to cut costs. Someone who cares about getting a job done in a timely way is unlikely to be energized in a role that has no targets or measures of achievement. Fortunately, motivation is not necessarily generated by the task, but often by the *reason* for doing it. People put their energy toward achieving something that they perceive as worthwhile. Your role is to help them see why their role is important in terms of the bigger picture.

We've already talked about each person's driver being a consistent part of who they are in all aspects of their lives. Money doesn't function as a long-term motivator. It's not that people don't want money; more often than not, a salary gives us the motivation to *get* a job. But once we're employed, we all have a need to address the *want to* factor that is linked to purposeful work.

Psychologist Frederick Herzberg introduced the concept of job enrichment. He researched the factors that affect a person's motivation to work. He found that people work hard when they see that what they do makes a difference. Psychologists agree that one's desire to do something is linked to the desire to be the best at what matters most. This never ceases to be a potential source of energy. People want to believe that what they do matters. The energy is there, waiting to be tapped. Energy begets energy.

Don't Confuse Commitment with Compliance

Several years ago, I received a call from a client at a children's hospital. They didn't know what to do about one of their best surgeons who had a non-productive relationship with the nurses on his team. The nurses saw him as aggressive, arrogant, and intimidating. They complained about how the surgeon made their work environment stressful and unpleasant. He was summoned to a meeting with management and told that he had to change his behaviour or else. His response went something like this:

> *I don't come to work every day worried about how to make life easier for the nurses. I come to save the lives of kids. If the nurses have an issue with me, that's their problem. If you insist on changing my behaviour, I have no doubt that I could easily get a job elsewhere. I am a top-notch surgeon. I get results. My reputation is sound. And I contribute to the good reputation this hospital has earned.*

Here's the dilemma. The threat of losing his job didn't worry this surgeon. He could easily fulfill his self-worth elsewhere. He had an established reputation that would allow him to do so. What's the solution? Most would argue that he needed to change his behaviour. He just

Part Two: Team Leadership Competencies

needed to know why he should do it. And that *why* needed to be defined by what he valued, not by what others value.

The solution was as simple as stepping back to better understand why he behaved as he did. What did he care most about? Not his relationships with his nurses. He had more to worry about than how they were feeling. He cared about saving children's lives, his reputation, the reputation of the hospital, and the success of his work. Now, what were the risks to him if he chose not to change his behaviour? He needed to see these risks through his own eyes, not through the eyes of the hospital administration. The risks would have to address *his* interests. What if conflict on the team caused critical mistakes? What if a child died as a result? What would be the risk to his patients if the surgical team became dysfunctional? What about the risk to the hospital's reputation or to his reputation? Part of the solution was for him to better understand the risk to those things he cared about – why things needed to change for the benefit of all. The nurses also had to be a part of the solution. They needed to understand why their response to his behaviour risked the health and welfare of their patients. A change in perception on both sides only happens when there is an understanding of the underlying intent of each party and their shared interests. The bottom line was that patient care was extremely important to both parties – the surgeon *and* the nurses.

This situation turned out well for all. Sometimes people stay and give in when threatened with losing their job. They do as they are told. They become compliant. That's what you don't want. Compliance is not commitment. With compliance, a person does only as much as is required to keep their job. That's not even close to achieving their performance potential.

Robert Cialdini, author of the book *Harnessing the Science of Persuasion*, emphasizes the importance of identifying those things a person values – to think about what that person would personally view as a desirable reward. And remember that what you value may not be perceived as a reward by someone else, and what you might see as punishing, could be someone else's reward. As the old saying goes, "One man's trash is another man's treasure." Your job is to find out what is treasure in the eyes of your associates.

In his book *If It Ain't Broke... BREAK IT!*, psychologist Robert Kriegel tells a story about a VP of sales who was asked his opinion regarding what individuals make the best salespeople. The VP demonstrated his response with a flip chart. On one side, he listed the typical qualifications of skills, competencies, knowledge, and experience in the field. On the other side, he wrote "fire in the heart" and said, "if I had to make a choice, I'd choose someone with fire over someone with background, education – the works. People with fire are more motivated, more resilient, will work harder, and are more resourceful. I can show them the ropes and give them the sales manuals. But if people don't have fire in their heart, they won't go anywhere." Kriegel goes on to quote Charles Wang, founder of Computer Associates International, saying he hires his sales force on "drive and enthusiasm, not technical expertise. If you have it in your heart, we can put what you need in your head." Remember the importance of putting fire into the hearts of your associates.

An associate with fire in the heart will give you their best discretionary effort. So, to create and sustain the energy that's needed for maximum performance, start by asking questions designed to provide insight into each associate as an individual. The most insightful questions are the ones that increase awareness of each person's motivations, perceptions, and expectations in your work relationship.

Here are a few to get started:

- What's important to you in the work you do?

- What do you value most?

- What are your expectations of me as your team leader? From your perspective, what do I do well? Where can I improve?

- What does teamwork mean to you? What do you value most about being on our team?

- What areas of your job do you appreciate the most? What makes that work so rewarding?

- What areas of your job do you least appreciate? What makes that work so unrewarding?

- What do you believe is your most important contribution to our team?

- What does success look like to you? How can I best support you in achieving success?

- What strengths do you believe you bring to this role? By strengths, I mean what you believe you do well and value doing. What would you like to learn to do better? How would that serve you in this role?

- What would have to happen for you to be able to look back on your performance and say, "that was my best"?

Tap Into the Energy of Engagement

Ideally, your associates would come to work each day, being both able and willing to perform at their best. They would be engaged. As the following illustration shows, engagement is the product of two key ingredients: motivation plus competence. In other words, engagement is *will* plus *skill*.

The *willing to* part of job performance is connected to each person's driver. Your associates are willing when they believe that their efforts lead to valued outcomes. That's when they bring more energy to their work. If a person with *will* doesn't have the experience or skills to do the task well, coaching or training usually can bring them up to speed. But the same does not hold true in reverse. If a person has the capability to do the task but not the will, no amount of training gives them the drive to do something they don't see the value of.

Engagement Solutions

The following matrix demonstrates the importance of both motivation and competence and what's needed to facilitate performance potential.

COMPETENCY #6: FACILITATE PERFORMANCE POTENTIAL

Engagement Solutions

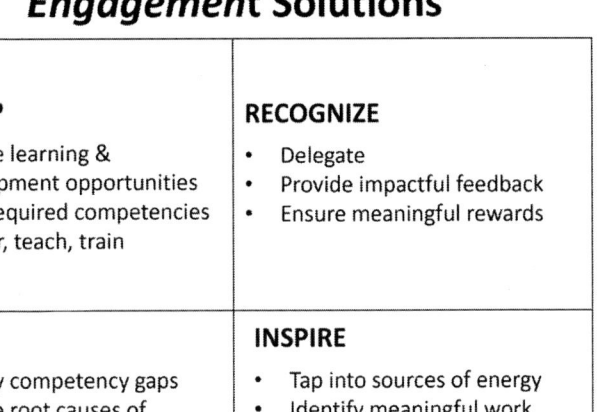

When motivation and/or competence are low, here are some potential solutions:

- When someone has *high motivation* (will) and *low competency* (skill), *develop* their skills and abilities through mentoring, teaching, and training.

- When someone has *low motivation* (will) and *high competency* (skill), *inspire* them by seeking to understand their sources of energy.

- When someone has *low motivation* (will) and *low competency* (skill), *assess* their performance gap and seek to understand what they need.

- When someone has *high motivation* and *high competency* (will + skill), this is the high engagement formula. *Recognize* them often and in meaningful ways.

Part Two: Team Leadership Competencies

Here are a few more ideas for how to engage your associates:

- When talking about objectives, refer to what's important to them.
    - If the person has the Drive for Achievement, emphasize what needs to be achieved and provide measurable outcomes.
    - If the person has the Drive for Affiliation, emphasize how they can provide a better service or help people, and allow them to do it.
    - If the person has the Drive for Autonomy, emphasize the importance of their expertise, and give them autonomy to apply it.
- When assigning roles, where possible, get people into tasks that align with their driver. Put yourself in their shoes. What might turn them onto or off that task? How could you describe their role's purpose in a way that appeals to their values? Create a motivating environment that matches what they value. If they value *achievement*, where can they take charge of a specific project with tangible results? If they value *affiliation*, what aspects of their work can include more interactions with others, or the opportunity to help? If they value *autonomy*, what can be done to allow them to work independently and be rewarded for their specific expertise?
- When discussing necessary tasks, connect them to their driver. Help them see the link between the outcomes of that work and what they value.
- When giving feedback, think about what feeds their self-worth. Everyone likes positive feedback; however, it needs to relate to their purpose. Recognize *results* for the achievement driver, *valuable service* for the affiliation driver, and *work quality* for the autonomy driver.

Most people are unaware of their driver. So, encourage them to look back at previous experiences and achievements. This gives them the opportunity to learn more about themselves. They benefit from reflecting on those times when their work was most satisfying – and, just as importantly, when it was not satisfying. When someone looks retrospectively, they have 20/20 vision. They develop a clear perception of their strengths – what they're good at, what they enjoy and value doing, what's most important to them, what keeps them engaged (gives them energy) and what disengages them (zaps their energy). You can ask them questions to help with their self-analysis: How do they like to go about fulfilling their role requirements? What causes stress and conflict for them? Memories all provide insight into those tasks that were meaningful and those that weren't.

If you want engaged and productive associates, build positive relationships with each of them. Be open to influence and honest in your communication. Seek to understand each person's perspective. Listen actively. Look for what motivates each person and what frustrates them. Demonstrate concern and earn their trust.

The Value of *Meaningful* Feedback

There's a common expression that refers to feedback as a gift. It's the information that enables a person to learn and grow. If you think giving feedback once a year, at the annual review, is sufficient, think again. You are missing opportunities for achieving peak performance. If you are interested in helping your associates reach their potential, it's critically important that you provide ongoing feedback.

At a national conference I attended many years ago, Ken Blanchard, author of *The One Minute Manager*, spoke about the importance of giving feedback. He related a story about the tendency for leaders to tell people only what they are doing wrong. He used an anecdote about a leader who takes the members of his team to a bowling alley and covers the pins before each person plays. The first team member takes a turn. After hearing the ball hit some pins, the leader calls out, "you missed three." Each team member that takes a turn hears about the pins they missed. They never hear about the pins they hit. The leader focused only on what they did wrong. Doing that usually results in defensiveness and anger. By contrast, some leaders are reticent to give negative feedback because they fear those emotional reactions, so they decide it's best not to give any feedback at all. That's not ideal either.

Part Two: Team Leadership Competencies

In his book, Blanchard emphasizes how important it is to catch someone doing things right. Tell them why it was important. Meaningful feedback goes beyond just saying "good job" or "that was great." It's about your perception of their actions and how they made a difference. Link it to what they value and ignite their energy. Without feedback, your associates won't know how they're doing or what they need to change to perform their best.

Meaningful Feedback Acknowledges Each Person's Value and Worth

Be specific and connect your feedback to each person's driver. "You did a great job" will have little impact without further specification. Make the connection by adding a specification: "You did a great job. I was particularly impressed with your ability to... [now fill in something that matches what they care about]." For example, "...to get it done in a tight time frame" would be meaningful to someone with the Drive for Achievement; "...to keep the team motivated and engaged" would be valued by a person who has the Drive for Affiliation; and "... to maintain the high standard we need" would resonate for an associate who has the Drive for Autonomy.

There will, of course, be times that you have to deliver negative feedback. Your associates want and need honest feedback, as long as it is given in a balanced way. Remember that strong emotions are always involved when the news isn't good. Feelings of inadequacy and self-doubt tend to surface. People become defensive, and when that happens, their perception narrows. All they hear is what they did wrong, and they remember only their failures and mistakes. That damages their sense of self-worth. Be sure to balance the losses with the wins. Past successes generate confidence and a more realistic view of strengths and weaknesses. Discuss what they do well, then move on to what needs to change.

Don't Forget, Feedback Works Both Ways

Honest feedback from your associates about *your* effectiveness as a leader is just as important as the feedback you give them. Just as your employees need to be aware of how you see them, you also benefit tremendously from knowing how they see you.

It's unrealistic to expect your associates to take the initiative and give you unsolicited feedback. They may be reticent to give you the feedback you need to learn and grow as a team leader. So, ask them for it! "What do I need to do to help you do your best?" "What's working in our relationship and what's not?" You also need to think about building trust in your work relationship. Do you see any signals that indicate potential problems? If so, have an honest and productive conversation about that. Your associates aren't likely to express their feelings openly. Invite them to do so and reap the benefit.

Rewards and Recognition Count Too!

Imagine a painting that an artist has created. It is that artist's unique creation. If a buyer of the painting only cares about the monetary value of the artist's work, it becomes a commodity that transcends the artist's talent. In the same way, if you only recognize the commodity side of your team members, the focus is primarily on what you pay them and what they're worth on the market.

Now think about the value they each bring to your relationship, your team and your organization. Focus on the uniqueness they bring. Their discretionary effort is linked to your recognition of this value. Every employee brings intrinsic strengths that add value. When you recognize those strengths, you feed that person's self-worth. Recognition is one of the strongest energizers. Feeling appreciated and recognized is powerful. If someone is recognized for the things that they value, you will continue to tap into their energy.

When it comes to rewards, *one size does not fit all*. It's important to match rewards to the receiver, not the giver. Don't fall into the trap of giving rewards that you yourself would value, thinking, "if I value it, why wouldn't someone else?" This thinking, of course, is flawed. You need to think about those distinct rewards that would suit individuals who care about different things. If people are rewarded in meaningful ways, they are more likely to be encouraged to continue to do the good work for which they are being recognized. It is not surprising that each team member views rewards differently. A person with the Drive for Autonomy may not respond positively to a bowling party as a reward for a successful team project. Some value quiet recognition for quality work; others prefer open recognition. Some look to tangible rewards, while others value personal notes of thanks. Some have no need for a thank-you because the quality of the work they produce is a reward in itself. Opportunities for more challenges are meaningful for some, while opportunities for new learning are more valuable to others. Use this principle to guide you. Understand that each reward has a different impact depending on what each person values.

Here are a few examples of meaningful rewards and recognition that align with each driver:

Drive for Achievement

- Opportunity to lead and direct people and projects
- Public recognition
- Acknowledgement for getting a job done
- Authority to take control, save time, complete a project
- Money
- Promotion or advancement opportunities

Drive for Affiliation

- Opportunity to help and support people
- Personal recognition
- Acknowledgement for making a difference
- The chance to improve work relationships
- Learning how efforts benefitted people
- Genuine words of thanks

Drive for Autonomy

- Opportunity to solve a problem or improve a product, process, or procedure
- Private recognition
- Acknowledgement for expertise and quality of work
- Tools to do the work; time to finish the work
- Trust in their competence
- Autonomy in decision-making

Learning Nuggets

This competency is made up of the skills required to ensure your associates achieve their performance potential.

Remember...

- ✓ Relationships are just as important as goals, objectives, and tasks.
- ✓ People always put more energy toward achieving something they see as worthwhile.
- ✓ Help your associates see why their role is important in terms of what they value, not what you value.
- ✓ Don't confuse commitment with compliance – do they *want to* do a task or feel they *have to*?
- ✓ Employee engagement requires both *will* and *skill* and what someone values, influences their degree of *will*.
- ✓ Ensure feedback, rewards and recognition are meaningful – match them to each person's driver to encourage them to do more.

You have now gained additional insight into engaging your team members. The next step is to look at your role in empowering them to apply the personal and interpersonal skills they need to manage their work relationships in productive ways. That's Competency #7, Coaching for Acuity.

COMPETENCY #7: Coach For Acuity

> *"I never cease to be amazed at the power of the coaching process to draw out the skills or talent that was previously hidden within an individual, and which invariably finds a way to solve a problem previously thought unsolvable."*
> —John Russell

Wouldn't it be great if your associates felt comfortable coming to you for guidance when faced with their work-related dilemmas? By dilemmas, I mean difficult situations, relationships that need to be more productive, personal/interpersonal conflicts, or any other problems that they are struggling to resolve. After all, these dilemmas don't tend to go away on their own, and they have a powerful impact on job performance. That's not good for your team.

Coaching for Acuity is not about becoming a coach, but about applying a coaching framework to guide people through a problem-solving process. You may think this takes too much time and energy. You are busy, and time is limited. However, as I've said before, conflict and stress-related issues have a way of escalating, especially when the root cause of a problem isn't addressed. Escalating problems become even more time-consuming in the long run. Very often, people don't have the skills or the self-awareness to resolve their own issues. Over time, their unresolved issues further damage their work relationships and diminish their performance. Think of Coaching for Acuity as a unique way for you to provide shared learning in order to keep your team members engaged and productive.

As you know, many personal and interpersonal issues stem from differing perspectives, values, and beliefs. You can share your Personal Leadership insights by guiding your associates toward seeing things from different points of view. Help them understand that they are not only part of the problem; they also must be part of the solution. Ultimately, they are accountable for the outcomes of their work relationships.

A Coach Is a Guide that Inspires Change

Most people don't understand that the issues they face cannot be separated from their perceptions, their beliefs, and their interactions. When personal and interpersonal dilemmas arise, they need to see the situation and the people involved from a different perspective. Think of a coaching conversation as your tool for positive action and change. You have the power to influence how your associates see themselves, how they see others, and how they create the outcomes they get. When someone's behaviours, however well-intended, interfere with getting the results they wanted, a key step toward change is for them to understand what drove them to behave that way. Without your guidance, your associates will most likely continue to see things from a narrow perspective and respond in the same way, getting the same results, again and again.

Now, if your goal is to inspire change, you might want to first look at yourself. Before engaging in a coaching conversation, reflect on the changes you, yourself, may need to make. Review your Personal Leadership competencies and identify any assumptions and beliefs that could be influencing your judgments of the people and the situations involved. Clarify any blind spots that might cloud your judgment.

Most organizations support the belief that managers should prescribe behaviours, exercise control, and fire employees who don't do what they're told. Think about how much advice you regularly receive – from your boss, your colleagues, or others. It usually starts with, "you know what you should do?" Now ask yourself, how often is that advice useful? If you said "not very," then you should be able to see that the same holds true for the advice you might be tempted to give your associates. Before you give advice, think about shifting from *controlling* to *enabling*.

Your goal is to guide someone toward greater self-awareness – to develop their capacity to move forward with commitment. Your job is not to tell someone what they should do or how they should do it. You want to help them generate insight and provide opportunities for reflection. As you might imagine, the quality of your listening in coaching conversations is as important as the content of what you say. Listening is your primary means for gaining commitment and leading a person toward change. Put listening ahead of your need to control. When you do, your associates will perceive you as someone willing to pay attention to what *they* believe is important. You might even learn something you didn't know before.

A coaching conversation is about leadership, not management. The focus is on creating something new. The intent is to engender trust and mutual respect. Trust reinforces that you have confidence in a person as a valued contributor. You acknowledge their perspective, skills, and accomplishments. Trust begets trust. When you demonstrate your trust in someone, they, in turn, trust you. Trust also comes from a focus on shared interests.

There is one important caveat to remember before entering a coaching conversation. Coaching only works if your associates take responsibility for their own actions and commit to change. The adage *you can lead a horse to water, but you can't force it to drink* aptly applies to coaching. No one can be coached unless they want to be. The motivation to participate in this process must come from them. There may be times when a person is simply not open to influence. They refuse to acknowledge that their challenges are inseparable from who they are, the way they think, and the way they act and interact with others. When that's the case, a coaching conversation isn't likely to change their perspective or behaviour. You may have no other option than to resort to disciplinary measures if and when an unresolved situation eventually impacts their performance and, potentially, that of the team.

People Don't Need to Be Managed... They Need to Be Understood

Learning is an essential component of change. So encourage your associates to reflect on past events in order to learn from experience. Reflection brings to light how a person interprets and makes meaning of their prior experiences. This is more than just looking back. It involves guiding them in closely examining their perceptions, assumptions, and behaviours. When you get them to challenge underlying assumptions and beliefs, they generate the change internally, rather than have it pushed on them by you. The value of insight far outweighs discipline. Don't focus on what you know or believe to be the right thing to do. Guide someone toward seeing things differently. You might not only get them to see things your way, but it's also very possible that you might change your perspective too.

Generate Self-Insight

To appreciate and lead each associate, you need to raise their awareness of themselves. Help them learn the impact of their intrinsic driver, their intentions, and their actions. This is an important first step to coaching someone. There's a learning loop of motivation, perception, actions, and outcomes that they must see in order to identify for themselves what needs to change. Engage them fully in understanding the link between their drive for self-worth and the outcomes they achieve.

It is vital that you help your associates understand the importance of personal self-insight, which goes hand-in-hand with confidence. Without confidence, people never reach their fullest potential. And with self-insight comes choice. Help your team develop the confidence to choose different ways of responding, reframing their actions in ways that are more in line with their intent.

Helping an associate build self-insight starts with guiding them to understand how their driver impacts everything they do and say – both actions and reactions. Help them become mindful of their preferred responses in different situations and the impact those responses have on others. Without this self-awareness, your associates won't understand why they respond to people and situations in certain ways and what they need to do differently to get a better result.

Transform Problems into Solutions

Have you ever noticed how people often spend time and energy grumbling about their situation rather than envisioning where they need to go and how to get there? When you help your associates create a picture of a future state, they stop looking at problems and see opportunities. Opportunities exist in a future state – a *desired* state that is uniquely defined by each person. When a person's current state is no longer acceptable, creating a picture of the desired state is critical. They've reached the point where they want and need things to be different and better. The tension created by the gap between the current and desired states is the fuel that mobilizes initiative and action.

A gap analysis is a visual way to help your associates close the gap between their current and desired states.

Part Two: Team Leadership Competencies

GAP ANALYSIS
ROOT CAUSE: WHY THE GAP
INTERVENTION: HOW TO CLOSE THE GAP

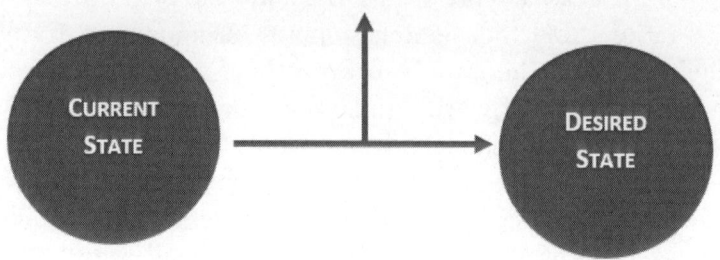

When engaging in gap analysis, help your associate identify the *why,* the *what,* and the *how* of the issue they are facing.

✓ Why is there the need to change?
✓ What specifically needs to be addressed?
✓ How will you get to where you need to be?

The Conversation: Hindsight + Foresight = Insight

You can have some powerful conversations with your people to inspire and generate change. These require both hindsight and foresight. *Hindsight* is the lens through which your associate learns more about themselves. It's about looking in the rear-view mirror for the insight that comes from experience. Typical hindsight questions include:

- What went well/what didn't go well?
- Why do you think you were successful/not successful?
- What did you learn? What are your takeaways?
- What were your major challenges and why?

Foresight is the lens through which your associate envisions what they need and why it's important to them. It's about reflecting on what the future might look like. Typical foresight questions include:

- What is your desired outcome?
- How do your insights apply?
- What needs to change?
- What will you do differently?

COMPETENCY #7: COACH FOR ACUITY

When you think about some of the most engaging conversations you've had, you probably did most of the talking and felt like someone else was really listening to you. This applies to coaching conversations, too: you need to do less talking and more listening. And when you do talk, be sure to be asking thoughtful questions that provoke reflection, insight, and action.

Judge yourself on the following criteria for a productive coaching conversation. Ideally, you'd place a check mark beside most of these statements. If you don't, note those that you haven't checked, and be mindful of those behaviours in future conversations.

- ☐ I focus on the quality of the relationship I have with my associate
- ☐ I seek to understand what drives that person
- ☐ I continue to be curious when I need to learn more
- ☐ I suspend my need to provide a solution for the problem
- ☐ I focus on asking the right questions, not giving the right answers
- ☐ I am sincerely interested in what my associate has to say – their perspective
- ☐ I admit when I don't understand something and ask for clarification

Remember that, in a coaching conversation, your associate most probably looks at things differently than you do. Be careful not to make the unconscious assumption that you both see the world the same way. When you tell someone what you would do, you're really saying that's what they *should* do, and that could be an incorrect assumption on your part. Before you start, be sure to hold aside your own beliefs about the situation. This allows you to better prepare your associate for solving the dilemma for themselves.

Part Two: Team Leadership Competencies

The DRIVE for Insight – A Coaching Conversation Process

I have found the *DRIVE* acronym to be helpful in leading coaching conversations.

D: Dilemma – What is the existing situation?

What's the current issue – the real challenge to be addressed? At this point, don't be quick to assume you know the reason for the issue or rush to suggest a potential solution. Probe for as much information as possible. Stick to facts, not opinions or assumptions. Find out what your associate has experienced, who's involved, when it has occurred, and how often.

R: Reflection – Why is it important?

Reflection leads to insight. This step is about becoming more mindful. What does your associate really want? What is the motivation behind the desired outcome?

- **Ask powerful questions.** Ask, don't tell. This is not the time to give advice. "You know what you should do?" doesn't belong here. People are more apt to act when they're working with their own ideas. Your advice is probably based on incorrect assumptions, in any case, so avoid "should" statements at all costs. You may think you know what your associate needs, but that tends to be based on *your* perception of what *you* might need under the same circumstances. Asking questions enables your associate to reflect further on the root cause of their dilemma. Use *what*, *why*, and *how* questions. "What's important here? Why is it so important to you? What impact is this dilemma having on you? How committed are you to resolving this issue? What are the consequences if you do nothing? How can you make this happen?"

- **Listen for Understanding.** Build a habit of curiosity. Listen for what the person is saying and what they're not saying. Listen for underlying emotions and the meaning behind their words. Ask yourself, "what's really going on?" Let them know you have listened. Ask questions to clarify what you've heard, and restate their points in your own words to show you've captured the essence of what they've said.

I: Insight – Why is it happening?

What are the triggers and contributing factors? Why does this problem exist in the first place? Help your associate come to an "a-ha" moment. Some dilemmas involve conflicting values. For example, your associate might need to achieve a goal within a tight time frame, and getting it done on time may require that they let go of their need for precision and accuracy. Your role, in this case, would be to help your associate reconcile these two competing values. Another example might involve an associate experiencing an interpersonal conflict with a colleague who demonstrates different intrinsic strengths. Your role then would be to provide additional insight into the potential reasons why those differences exist.

V: Vision – What does the solution look like?

Help your associate imagine their desired future, asking, "What will it look like if this dilemma is resolved?" A vision of the future provides a shift in perspective, leading toward creative problem-solving. A vision generates positive energy that can be used to identify the steps to get to a successful outcome. It moves your associate from focusing on "what's not working" to "what's possible." Ask insightful questions and explore potential solutions.

E: Engagement – How can they achieve the desired state?

Energize the associate for action. Consider what would happen if nothing were done to resolve the dilemma. Re-connect to their purpose – the reason why, from *their* perspective, the dilemma needs to be resolved. Get their commitment to a solution. Finally, guide them toward choosing the best actions to achieve it. Ensure they are committed to these actions, and be sure to follow up to see how they're progressing.

Learning Nuggets

This competency is made up of the skills required to conduct coaching conversations that help your associates resolve their personal and interpersonal dilemmas.

Part Two: Team Leadership Competencies

Remember ...

- ✓ A coaching conversation is a powerful way to inspire and generate change.
- ✓ Coaching generates insight and provides opportunities for reflection.
- ✓ Increase someone's self-insight, and you'll build their potential to make better choices.
- ✓ Better problem-solving comes from seeing things from different angles.
- ✓ When someone understands why they do what they do, they can generate ideas for what to do differently the next time around.

When your associates experience the learning that comes from coaching conversations, the result is a collective group that works cohesively and shares a common purpose. This brings us to Competency #8, Build Cohesive Teams.

COMPETENCY #8: BUILD COHESIVE TEAMS

"Coming together is a beginning. Keeping together is progress. Working together is success." —Henry Ford

In a September 2020 Forbes article titled "How to Get The Best From Each Team Member – Including Yourself," contributor Liz Kislik wrote, "Today's challenges can be deeply draining, and many people are working harder than ever to keep up with the many current uncertainties. But if leaders are willing to invest in getting to know all their team members for who they are and help them find consonance by aligning their responsibilities with their personal values, there's a much greater chance for both employees and organizations to experience growth and success together."

If you want to ensure that each member of your team is engaged and contributes maximum discretionary effort, then you must create a cohesive team culture where all members respect and value the different strengths and perspectives in the group.

No one can argue that a team needs to be aligned on what it needs to achieve – its mandate, goals, and objectives. Obviously, there needs to be clarity of roles and a shared vision. However, for peak performance, you need more than that. Working with many teams has provided me with a valuable lesson that teams also need to be cohesive in order to be most productive. You can bring the best-qualified people together into a work group, but if they can't work together as a cohesive unit, they won't achieve their performance potential.

Healthy Relationships Are the Hallmark of a Cohesive Team

On a cohesive team, disagreements never become personal, and conflict is prevented. When team members do experience conflict, they feel comfortable sharing what they think and how they feel, and they are mindful of doing so in respectful ways. They are confident that their perspective will be heard and, most importantly, understood. Even if no one else agrees with their point of view, they will have the opportunity to voice an opinion and listen to an exchange of views, opinions, values, and ideas. Cohesion means each team member understands and respects the strengths and perspectives of their colleagues. They listen actively and respond constructively to different points of view. There is high trust, constructive debate, and energy to get things done. Doesn't that sound like a team you would like to lead?

As the team leader, check the statements below that you believe to be true for you. Each statement is a leadership practice that helps to build cohesion:

- ☐ I encourage a climate of mutual respect and honest communication
- ☐ I listen to diverse perspectives before I speak
- ☐ I recognize the importance of each associate based on their role on the team
- ☐ I note behaviours in meetings – associates who are constantly outspoken and who consume airtime, and those who remain quiet – then I seek to understand why
- ☐ I prevent disagreements from becoming personal, focusing on the facts, not the person
- ☐ When an associate disagrees with me or others, I put myself in their shoes; I try to see things from their perspective
- ☐ I never react or make judgments before understanding a person's *why*

Note which statements that you didn't check off. Try to incorporate those actions into your team-leadership practices.

Relationships and Purpose are Team Essentials

Relationships between team members have the potential to make or break your team's performance. So building cohesion is the best way to prevent many of the conflicts that arise between people with different perspectives. When conflicts inevitably arise, a cohesive team is better equipped to manage and resolve those conflicts in constructive ways.

Your team produces both task and social outcomes. Task outcomes relate to the achievement of a team's goals and objectives, while social outcomes relate to the way your team members interact. Positive social outcomes are the signals of healthy relationships on a team. Two similar teams could achieve the same task results with completely different social outcomes. On one team, the interactions might be visibly unpleasant, showing signs of stress and conflict – tempers flaring, avoidance of each other, or passive aggression. The other team might demonstrate cooperation, collaboration, tolerance, and mutual respect. That's the team that's going to be most productive in the long run. That's the group that's investing in their interpersonal relationships – otherwise known as their *social capital*.

American sociologist James Coleman was the first to develop the concept of social capital. The term refers to the functioning of social groups. A group with high social capital is characterized by a spirit of trust, cooperation, and reciprocity. When you increase your team's social capital, you increase its capability to get the work done. In today's high-stress environments, social capital has become more important than ever. As a team leader, you play a critical role in fostering a culture of trust with and between team members.

A cohesive team works together like a tightly woven fabric. People are accountable for working together productively and preventing conflict. Without cohesion, things don't get done as easily or as quickly as they could. Draw your team's attention to any non-productive behaviours that you or others have perceived. That includes hidden agendas, angry outbursts, projection of blame, and avoidance of personal accountability. These non-productive behaviours lead to mistrust, conflict, faulty assumptions, and impulsive reactions that result from a lack of reflection on the situation and people involved. By comparison, productive behaviours include collaborative problem-solving, honest dialogue, cooperation, and respect for diversity.

Reflect on what's working well and what's not working well on your team. Are all team members clear on the team's purpose? If you were to ask people to communicate their perception of the team's purpose, would their answers be the same? If there are differences in perception, is there discussion regarding these differences? Do team members understand why those differences exist?

Diversity is a Good Thing

It's important that individual differences be welcomed and valued on a team. Sometimes people believe that differences can only lead to disagreements and conflicts. Help your team understand that proactive, open discussion about differences has the power to change how they see things. It prevents the escalation of conflict and opens the door to mutually beneficial solutions. Every team member has a stake in keeping the team's relationships healthy and productive.

Rules of engagement define how a team agrees to work together. When there are rules, team members feel more confident addressing behaviours that break those rules. It's always hard to argue with your own data.

Here's an example of a set of rules that I developed with a client organization. How might these work for your team?

We each have the right to...

- ✓ Express our personal perspective
- ✓ Be heard and respected

We each have a responsibility to...

- ✓ Respect individual differences
- ✓ Focus on strengths, not weaknesses
- ✓ Listen with an open mind
- ✓ Prevent conflict

We demonstrate respect for each other when we...

- ✓ Seek to understand every viewpoint
- ✓ Actively listen when someone speaks
- ✓ Give constructive feedback rather than vent
- ✓ Acknowledge different perspectives and ways of doing things

We demonstrate concern for each other's well-being when we...

- ✓ Address issues or concerns respectfully
- ✓ Create a safe environment to speak
- ✓ Clarify our assumptions of intent

COMPETENCY #8: BUILD COHESIVE TEAMS

Be Mindful When Hiring

When you hire new team members, consider the influence of your driver. I worked with a team of people who all valued affiliation. The leader admitted that she tended to hire people like her. She was more focused on the individual person she was interviewing than on the skills needed to round out her team. Unfortunately, team results suffered. The members were too alike. They enjoyed working together, but their collegiality came at the expense of task accomplishment. No one, not even the leader, was comfortable making a tough decision or honestly pointing out that time was wasted in their never-ending meetings.

Be careful that you don't fall into the same trap and hire only team members who are just like you. If you only hire in your own image, you're forfeiting the opportunity to be influenced by different perspectives. Remember, you're not hiring someone for the job *you* do, but for a different role, one that may require entirely different strengths. Be mindful of this hiring bias, or you may end up with a group of people that all do the same things in the same way and for the same reason. Who fills in the gaps?

Differences on a team bring a variety of perspectives and strengths. For example, it could serve you well when there are some members who prevent things from coming to a standstill when there's all talk and no action, some who prevent conflict when the spirit of cooperation is missing, and some who prevent mistakes when agendas are moving too quickly.

Think of your group of associates. How do you see their behaviour? What do you believe is important to each individual? What do they care about? What might be some potential sources of stress or conflict? What are their sources of energy? You need to leverage each person's driver to harness the group's collective strengths.

Make sure everyone agrees on what a high-performing team looks like and how your team should operate. If you ask each team member, you may be surprised by the different perspectives you hear. These different opinions are rarely expressed, which can lead to some team members becoming frustrated when the team doesn't meet their own expectations. I once got frustrated on a team that wasn't meeting my expectations. At a team meeting, I shared my perspective that a high-performing team is one where there is open dialogue, mutual support, and shared learning and that I wasn't experiencing this behaviour on our team. One colleague immediately disagreed. She reminded me that there are many definitions of a team. From her perspective, we were a ski team, not a hockey team – and the other team members agreed. That was a lightbulb moment for me. My expectations were different than those of others. And that was important to know. I felt at odds with the majority, but I was also relieved. With this additional insight, I felt less frustrated. When a team's culture doesn't inspire, every person on that team always has the choice to stay and adapt, or to leave. I chose to adapt for the short term, but left within the year.

A Team Is a Group with Shared Purpose

Regardless of whether or not members agree on what a productive team looks like, everyone needs to be committed to a collective sense of purpose. It's the glue that holds everyone together, and it must be understood and valued by all members of the team. When there's a clear purpose, there's more than just a focus on tasks: everyone sees the bigger picture and the reason why the team exists.

Task accomplishment, service, and quality are all important components of a common purpose, and you may find differences in opinion regarding which of those components is most important. Imagine a group of individuals with diverse drivers. Despite their differences, they have a common purpose. If someone has the Drive for Achievement, they may see getting the task done as priority one. If someone has the Drive for Affiliation, they might consider delivering on service expectations most important. If someone has the Drive for Autonomy, quality of work output often takes precedence for them.

As an illustration, imagine a project team responsible for overseeing the move of a manufacturing facility to a new location. At one of their team meetings, different perspectives arise.

- Jane is focused on how the team needs to make quicker decisions in order to meet their deadline date. She's frustrated that there's too much talk and not enough action.

- Frank is concerned that some people will have to relocate or face longer commutes to work. He's worried about the impact on morale and team performance and wants to discuss "what-if" scenarios.

- Carrie wants to slow things down to ensure that previous mistakes are avoided this time around. It's most important to her that they clarify project milestones and mitigate risks.

Each person feels their concerns are the most valid. They start to debate the importance of their own points of view. The overall team purpose becomes lost. Although they share the same objective to get the project done, within budget, and on time, neither Frank nor Carrie believes that the objective should be attained at the expense of something they deem more important. For Frank, it's employee morale. For Carrie, it's risk management.

In this case, each team member needs to understand how another perspective has value, to see things from a different point of view. What is the cost of ignoring morale or making mistakes that result in increased times and costs? It's all important. The question the team should be asking, collectively, is, "How can we meet the need to finish on time while ensuring people are considered and risks are managed?"

The Tuckman Model of Team Development

Even a team that works together productively experiences changing circumstances that can impact its relationships. In 1964, researcher Dr. Bruce Tuckman published the *Tuckman's Stages of Group Development*. This theory is still relevant today. Tuckman identified four distinct phases of team development: Forming, Storming, Norming, and Performing. Each stage has a common set of interpersonal dynamics and is an inevitable part of a team's evolution. Let's look at Tuckman's model as it relates to the concepts in this book.

Part Two: Team Leadership Competencies

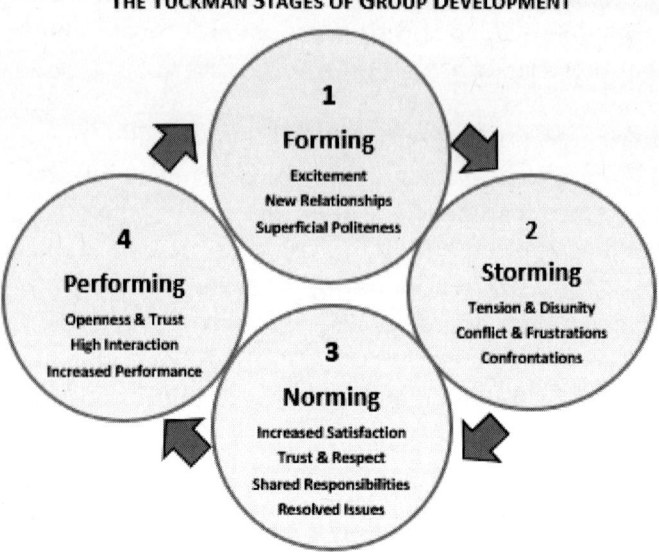

As you review each stage in detail, reflect on where your team might be and consider some of the suggested actions.

1. Forming

If your team is in this stage of development, *building awareness* needs to be your focus. They will be highly dependent on you for guidance and direction. At the start, individual roles and responsibilities are unclear; be prepared to clarify them. Answer questions about the team's purpose. At this stage, team members need to understand each other from a relationship perspective. Give individual team members the chance to share their unique perspectives and values. The desired outcome is the acceptance of each other.

Recognize that relationships are still unknown in this stage of development. This is the time they are formed, along with first impressions. You may observe less open communication, as team members are often reticent to speak about issues and concerns in these early days. Schedule frequent team meetings and focus on building trust. It's the cornerstone of productive relationships. Provide opportunities for team members to get to know one another. Allow people to introduce themselves to each other. Ask each person to share what they would like to personally achieve as a member of the team, and what is personally important to them about their role and its contribution to the purpose of the team.

Make sure you clearly define the role of each team member. Without role clarification, conflict is inevitable and there can be duplication of effort. People won't understand the boundaries of authority and responsibility. There is no clear distinction between what they have the authority to do and what must be approved by someone else. This often leads to inaction, frustration, and confusion.

2. Storming

If your team is in this stage of development, *handling divisiveness* should be your primary focus. What we often see in this stage is blaming, competitiveness, and conflict. Your challenge is to manage disagreements. Address conflict and enable people to reach consensus in a positive way. Don't ignore it. Mediate when required. This is a critical stage in your team's development, and it's also the most challenging. As we discussed earlier, managing *opposition* requires an understanding of the *issues*, while managing *conflict* requires an understanding of the *people*.

This is especially important at this stage of the team's development. People have strong views on what's right and what's wrong. Emotions run high when someone appears to disregard what's important to someone else and makes no attempt to understand the other person's perspective.

Think about your team's current reality and how each team member looks at the situations they encounter. Is the team experiencing a lot of change? If so, provide the opportunity for each person to describe what causes conflict for them during change. Ask them how they feel when they see someone doing what they believe is the wrong thing. This technique can apply to many different situations. Discuss what each team member sees as most important in the delivery of effective client service. Is your team working on a specific project? If so, how do they see a project management process working most effectively? Do they agree on the definition of their team? Do they have different opinions regarding how they should work together? In other words, a good way to understand conflict on your team is to learn what creates conflict for people when they see things being done the "wrong" way from their perspective. Encourage team members to share their answers to the questions posed.

Part Two: Team Leadership Competencies

It's especially important during this stage that each team member adopt the *listen to learn* perspective. Encourage active listening so that the group can express and understand diverse viewpoints.

Often, when there's conflict, team members try to avoid one another. If you see this happening, allow some time to put relevant issues on the table. Never focus on what's wrong with someone or who's to blame. Help people discuss the root causes of conflict objectively so that they can design a plan to resolve it. Because conflict has the potential to escalate to the point where relationships are damaged, this is a good time to guide your team toward developing rules of engagement. Encourage your team to develop proactive strategies while still engaged in solving problems for mutual gain.

3. Norming

If your team is in this stage of development, your focus now shifts to *sustaining cohesion*. What we often see here are more appropriate behaviours, more interactive dialogue, and open discussion of issues – strengthened unity. The team is functioning well and getting the work done. There is no visible or hidden conflict. What you might observe is that there's not much excitement or energy. You might be tempted to be pleased about the acceptable levels of discretionary effort. However, there's still some room for improvement in productivity and job satisfaction. Your desired outcome of this stage is to generate the energy to achieve even higher levels of performance.

How can you keep energy high? How do you keep the team from falling into a state of complacency? Ask them to come up with new challenges to take them out of their comfort zones. With new challenges, people get the energy needed to do their best. Provide new development opportunities. Find out what people would value learning for their personal and professional growth. Encourage innovation, doing things differently. Finally, provide feedback about what they're doing right. Recognize the team for what's going well. People want to feel valued. When you praise and recognize more often, you increase the likelihood that the team will move to the next stage.

4. Performing

If your team is in this stage of development, your focus should be on *sustaining momentum* and achieving peak performance. In this stage, there is energy, a strong sense of shared purpose, and high levels of trust between team members and with you. To sustain momentum, celebrate successes in meaningful ways. Consider switching your leadership style from directing to facilitating. Maintain drive and energy by enabling people to accomplish things that continue to contribute to their intrinsic driver.

How Cohesive Is Your Team?

Take a closer look at your current team culture. Is there trust and open communication? What are your team members perceiving? How do your team members see you as the leader? How do you show up? Remember, whatever your associates perceive, that's *their* reality, not yours.

There are as many different interpretations of situations as there are team members. As I've said, no two people see the world the same way. Remember the Rashomon effect that emphasizes this point. Put ideas and issues on the table to discover how people attach different meanings to things. This allows you to clearly see how people differ in their interpretations of the same thing. Stay open to different reactions. Don't immediately look for allies that support what you believe is important or label people as resistors. Expect diverse opinions. Be open to challenges to existing practices.

Prevent conflict, don't avoid it. When it does happen, move it onto the table – bring it into the open. Remember, conflict isn't always visible. Allow team members to surface the issues they may be reticent to share because they fear retaliation. Make sure they know it's okay to disagree in respectful ways.

Your Team Cohesion Index

Here's an index to check your team's cohesion. Place a check mark beside each statement that's true for your team. The number of check marks indicates the degree to which your team is cohesive.

Part Two: Team Leadership Competencies

____ Team members understand each other; they value different drivers and strengths

____ Everyone deals with issues in a direct and constructive way

____ Team members openly discuss concerns and don't remain silent to avoid potential conflict

____ Differences of opinion are tabled with productive dialogue and healthy debate

____ Disagreements stay objective and impersonal

____ Everyone has a sense of unity around everything they do

____ Everyone operates with a clear understanding of their individual roles and accountabilities

____ Team members are aware of how their roles connect to our team's vision

____ Team members are aligned around common goals

____ Team members understand their contribution to the overall purpose of our team

Review the statements where you did not put a check mark. You may want to discuss these statements at your next team meeting. If trust is high on your team, you could also ask each member to complete this exercise, note the differences in their responses, and discuss the results.

Learning Nuggets

This competency is made up of the skills required to create a cohesive team with a culture of trust and mutual respect.

Remember...

✓ Model the behaviours you expect of all team members.

✓ Recognize people in ways that build their self-worth – leverage each person's intrinsic driver and strengths.

COMPETENCY #8: BUILD COHESIVE TEAMS

- ✓ Acknowledge different perspectives. Build a team that values trust and mutual respect.
- ✓ Move conflict out from under the table – prevent it, don't avoid it.
- ✓ Create a climate of open dialogue and constructive debate.

Together, Personal and Team Leadership competencies maximize the performance potential of your team. Now read on to see how the remaining two Team Leadership competencies further build your capability to resolve interpersonal conflicts and to guide people through change.

COMPETENCY #9: MEDIATE CONFLICTS

"Every fight is one between different angles of vision, illuminating the same truth."
—Mahatma Gandhi

Even the most cohesive team experiences conflicts between team members. Mediating conflict is not the same as being a professional mediator. As the team leader, your role is more complex than that. A professional mediator needs to be objective, impartial, and removed from the issues of a dispute, but it's difficult to remain objective when you're the team leader. You're never a neutral party in a dispute between members of your team, because you have a stake in the outcome.

Constructive Debate Is Better Than Conflict

There are bound to be conflicting viewpoints and misunderstandings on your team that lead to more serious conflicts. Your goal is to ensure that your associates replace potentially harmful conflict with constructive debate. Conflicts are costly. They can result in reduced productivity, poor work quality, absenteeism, disciplinary problems, and increased turnover. Take the time to not only prevent these conflicts but resolve them when they occur. We experience harmful conflict as highly personal and emotional. When someone feels misunderstood, ignored, or unfairly treated, that's emotional. Perhaps you can recall feeling frustrated, anxious, or angry in situations where others have ignored or devalued what is important to you. Remember how difficult it was to focus on a resolution when you became emotional? On the other hand, if you were engaged in a constructive debate, I'll bet it felt less emotional. Constructive debate transforms conflict into a disagreement that, when mediated, leads toward positive change. People behave differently when they are given the opportunity to understand different perspectives. We generate new ideas when we take the time to listen to dissenting points of view in respectful ways. In a constructive debate, conflicts are addressed, not suppressed. When you lead your associates through this more positive process, you automatically open the lines of communication. Your associates will talk *to*, rather than *about*, each other.

Common Misconceptions

Take a close look at how conflict is viewed on your team. Is it seen as a threat or an opportunity? If your associates see it as a threat, then their first instinct may be to deny or avoid it. On the other hand, if they see it as an opportunity, they will likely be open to constructive debate, creative problem-solving, and mutually agreed-upon solutions.

Let's look at some common misconceptions about conflict that you may need to clarify for your team.

- **"If I ignore it, it will go away."** If you ignore conflict, the root cause continues to simmer, like a forest fire that burns underground, waiting for the right circumstances to reignite. The fire continues because the source has not been extinguished. Ignoring conflict is not a solution. If it's ignored, the conflict tends to just escalate. And when that happens, relationships can be irreversibly damaged.

- **"Anger is a destructive emotion that doesn't belong in the workplace."** Anger is, in fact, a human emotion that is neither positive nor negative. We express it when strong reactions are sparked in us. It presents us with an opportunity to find its root cause and deal with it. When people aren't committed or don't care about an issue, they don't experience anger. The opportunity to express anger in safe ways allows others to understand where someone is coming from, resolve a conflict, and move forward, rather than allowing it to simmer below the surface.

- **"Conflict should be resolved as quickly as possible."** Unfortunately, any rush toward a resolution usually ends up with short-term results. If you've resolved conflict quickly, it's likely that you've missed some important information or addressed the symptoms rather than the root cause. Predictably, the conflict will return.

- **"People in conflict aren't committed to their team."** Conflict occurs when people have strong beliefs and opinions about what's important to them. If they didn't care, they wouldn't put their energy into the conflict. Conflict serves as the tool to expose what each person genuinely cares about.

Part Two: Team Leadership Competencies

Sources of Conflict on Your Team

The sources of conflict are diverse. Often, they relate to the human reaction to change. Ronald Heifetz and Marty Linsky, authors of *Leadership on the Line: Staying Alive Through the Dangers of Leading*, define two major types of challenges in change: technical and adaptive. Technical challenges are defined as those that can be solved by experts. With technical challenges, the problem, the solution, and the implementation are clear. Adaptive challenges, on the other hand, require changes in values, beliefs, roles, relationships, and approaches to work. People often resist these changes because the solutions can't be implemented by a project plan. And, when adaptive changes are not addressed, they can generate conflict.

Heifetz has said, "the single biggest failure of leadership is to treat adaptive challenges like technical problems. Technical changes can be listed on a plan and checked off at each milestone. But how do you create milestones related to changes in perceptions, values, and beliefs?"

The way to resolve conflict generated by adaptive change is to get to the root causes that are emotional, not rational. I once worked with a senior marketing team in a manufacturing organization. The company had recently been acquired. After the acquisition, technical changes came quickly for the team; new roles, responsibilities, reporting relationships, and work processes were introduced. The adaptive challenges, on the other hand, proved more difficult for the team to manage. Team members differed in how they viewed the changes and the challenges they faced. Some adapted more easily than others. Some saw growth opportunities while others saw losses. Relationships became tenuous. Team members became either active supporters or resisters.

The resulting conflict became visible. There were shouting matches in the hallways. At the team's first session with me, one member approached me privately to confirm how excited she was by the changes, while another team member took me aside to share how terrible things had become. They were different people with different viewpoints, each believing that their perspective was right. When this happens, the only solution is to provide the time needed for the team to engage in a facilitated dialogue. Each team member needed to have the opportunity to speak safely and openly about their concerns, and everyone on the team needed to hear every perspective.

Preventive vs. Prescriptive Solutions... Which Do You Prefer?

Your goal is to help your associates find a mutual solution that resolves their conflict and prevents it from reoccurring. You may be tempted to seek quick-fix solutions based on what you see happening around you. But remember that when you see overt anger, over-reactions, personal attacks, ongoing disagreements, low trust, a decline in productivity, or the forming of divisive cliques, you are observing the symptoms of something simmering beneath the surface.

Prescriptive solutions focus only on the symptoms – your early warning signs. When you only address symptoms, it's likely that the conflict won't go away. If you don't uncover the cause of the conflict, there's a risk that the real issue will escalate to an even more serious level.

Preventive solutions, on the other hand, are designed to address hidden, underlying root causes. They lead to longer-term resolutions that prevent the conflict from returning.

Addressing the symptoms of conflict leads to *prescriptive*, short-term solutions that allow the conflict to resurface.

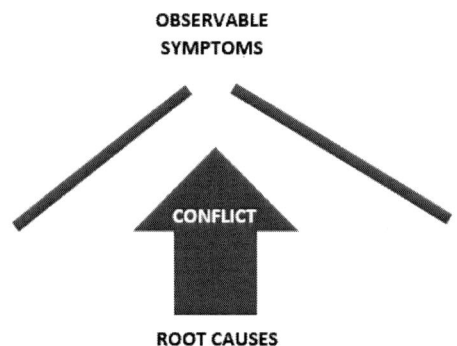

Addressing the underlying causes of conflict leads to *preventative*, longer-term solutions that eliminate the conflict.

Part Two: Team Leadership Competencies

Barriers to Resolving Interpersonal Conflicts

In their book, *Difficult Conversations: How To Discuss What Matters Most,* Douglas Stone, Bruce Patton, and Sheila Heen show how conflict is always more complex than it appears. In particular, the authors discuss the important distinction between *telling messages* and *learning conversations.* Conflict resolution requires that people shift from a framework of proving to a framework of understanding. It's important to guide your associates away from the need to prove they're right, toward a willingness to understand someone else's viewpoint and to learn something new.

MESSAGE FRAMEWORK	LEARNING FRAMEWORK
Proving	Understanding

When people are stuck in a message framework, they want to prove that they are right and that the other person is wrong. They think to themselves, "I know all that I need to know. I just need to make sure the other person sees it my way." They make an assumption about another person's intent, even though intentions are invisible. They're interpreting what they see from their own narrow perspective, making it easy to cast blame. "The other person is the problem, not me. The fault is all theirs." When in a *proving* mode, people are no longer open to new learning. All their energy goes to defending their position.

Within a learning framework, assumptions are different. Each person assumes that they both have different perspectives on an issue. They know they're missing important information that will help them fully understand the situation. They acknowledge that they've each contributed to the conflict in some way.

Mediation improves relationships by creating a learning framework. Engaging your associates in a mediated conversation provides the opportunity for them to reconcile their differences with mutual understanding and respect. It provides a fresh lens through which to view the situation from a different angle.

Your primary purpose is to get your team members to share their perspectives and reach a mutually agreeable solution. Keep in mind that your task is not to solve their problem; it's to guide them toward reaching a resolution. A mediated conversation involves helping them understand different points of view, broadening their perception of an issue, diffusing the tension, empowering them to envision creative solutions, and supporting them in reaching their own conclusions. It's not likely that those involved in a dispute will become friends or even grow to like one another. That's not your goal. They just need to be able to work together productively.

To resolve a conflict in a mutually agreeable way requires active participation from those involved. Your associates must be accountable for the problems they are experiencing, they must commit to listening to different perspectives, and they must agree to this collective ownership of the problem.

Mediation 101

In any dispute, each person's intrinsic driver influences their perception of the facts. When facilitating a mediated conversation, focus on the problem, not the people. This is often a challenge. As conflict escalates, team members become entwined with the problem. Details become obscured and emotions cloud perceptions. Personal attacks occur when emotions flare. Steer discussions back to the facts, and make sure those facts are validated. Encourage both people to listen actively to better understand the underlying reasons for the issue. Help them discover why the other person is so emotionally involved.

Learning to think and act like a mediator is the same as learning to think and act like a coach. You can benefit from the skills and concepts of both coaching and mediation to guide your associates through difficult conversations. Remember, your own lens has an impact on what you see and hear. Always stay focused on separating facts from opinions. Be mindful of your own biases and engage in active listening. Don't argue with what someone else believes to be true.

Mediating conflicts includes three components – storytelling, interactive listening, and problem-solving. Your role is to help your associates understand that each component is important for achieving a mutually agreed resolution.

In mediation, *storytelling* is exactly what it sounds like. You want to encourage each person to tell their side of the story – to share their perspective and their intention, without interruption. Stories are personal perspectives. They bring to light information that is often unknown to other people. As the mediator, you set the rules for this process.

Part Two: Team Leadership Competencies

Encourage each person to share their own depiction of events, including what they assume to be true, what they deem important, and what they expect to see happen. While one person tells their story, the other person must listen. You may need to probe for further clarification to understand the meaning behind the words, perhaps by re-stating what you hear, saying, "It sounds like your concern is..." or "From my perspective, it looks like..." The goal is to make sure each person hears a personal perspective and learns something new.

As people share their perspectives, it's important that you encourage *interactive listening*. This is the second component. It's a form of listening that ensures that each person is both listening and learning. This means they must provide their undivided attention. To "attend" means to be present. Encourage face-to-face communication, eye contact, and the removal of any potential distractions, including negative feelings. Rather than listening to judge the other person, ask them to concentrate on what the other person is saying or feeling. They should be prepared to summarize their understanding of what they have heard. Interactive listening also requires that people feel safe to speak. If a person feels that what they say will be used against them in some way, they will be reticent to be open and honest. Simple ground rules can help in this regard. You might say, "What's said in this room, stays in this room," "There is no absolute right or wrong opinion here," or "Each person's point of view is valid and worthwhile." Statements like this build trust and encourage full disclosure on both sides.

Problem-solving is the third component and the key to ensuring that your associates attack the issue, not each other. It's important to separate the people from the problem. Personalities shouldn't enter the equation. Problem-solving requires steering the focus toward interests, not positions. Interests represent what's important to each person concerning the issue, while a position is merely a person's perception of what they believe is the solution. Interests open the door to exploring any number of potential solutions that could meet the interests of both parties.

Interest-Based Problem-Solving Is Your Goal

Have you ever noticed when there are conflicts that people immediately say what they believe is the solution? We hear them say, "I know what we need to do," "The only way to tackle this is..." or "It's obvious what the problem is." When people take a position, they're projecting their own narrow perception of the situation and their interests. The way they see it, their position is the only solution. More often than not, it's not the best solution. It's only one possible solution out of many. When someone says, "We need to cut costs to increase profits," their *interest* is to increase profits, and their position is that cutting costs is the only way to go about doing it.

Interests get to the reason someone wants an outcome. This is an important point because people only experience conflict when someone or something has undermined what they care about. When you explore a person's interests, you get a window into what's important to them. It's their underlying motivation – their why. If you ask why someone believes something is necessary, that is, what's driving their suggestion, you'll get to their underlying interests. In conflict, understanding each person's underlying interests opens the door to any number of potential solutions.

There are both individual and joint interests. Joint interests represent the common ground. So you want to guide the discussion toward that common ground – that will lead to a solution that satisfies both parties, one that each person is likely to commit to. When joint interests are uncovered, each person willingly contributes options that represent acceptable solutions.

The Mediation Process

The earlier you engage in a mediation process, the better the outcome. If the conflict hasn't escalated to a more serious level, it is much more likely that the people involved will commit to solving the problem. Guide the conversation using the following components of interest-based problem-solving:

Ground rules: Ensure both sides are committed to working collaboratively to achieve a solution that meets the needs of both parties. Each party must agree to:

- Be engaged in resolving the dispute with each other
- Respect confidentiality
- Demonstrate mutual respect
- Be sincere and honest; focus on both facts and feelings
- Be open-minded
- Be willing to separate the person from the problem

Initial storytelling: Allow each person to tell their story from their own perspective. Ask, "Why are we here today?" "What's the situation, from your point of view?" "Why is this important to you?" "Is there anything else that you would like _____ (the other person) to know, to ensure that they understand your perspective?"

Individual and shared interests: Separate wants (interests) from beliefs (positions). Summarize what you've heard. Say, "This is what I've heard about what's important to each of you," and "These are your shared interests…"

Identification of issues and obstacles: Remove what's standing in the way. Ask, "What's preventing you both from getting what you want?" "What needs to get resolved?" or "What needs to happen or be addressed today, to be successful?"

A joint problem question: A joint problem question addresses individual needs and joint interests. It must be positive and neutral in its language. For example, "How will this project be completed by the target date, while ensuring that risks are mitigated?" or "What really needs to be addressed today to have a satisfactory solution for you both?" Once the question is defined, ask, "If this question is answered, will we have resolved all of your issues today?"

When you have a solution that fully satisfies the needs of both parties, you have successfully mediated a dispute. This may require more than one meeting. Once there is understanding, clarity, and agreement, the mediation process closes. As a follow-up, it's always wise to meet with each person to ensure that the issue is, in fact, resolved.

Remember to use interactive listening to determine:

1. **The issue or problem** – What are the root causes?

2. **Individual interests** – What's important to each person? What is a conflict catalyst for each of them?

3. **Joint interests** – What's important to both of them?

4. **Viable options** – What are the potential solutions?

5. **Commitments** – Are solutions aligned with joint interests?

Also, remember to focus on dialogue, not debate. Refer to the following chart as a reminder of the difference between these two forms of communication. Shift each person's focus from an entrenched position to one of shared interests.

DEBATE	DIALOGUE
Listening for ammunition	Listening for understanding
Focused on *own* ideas	Focused on *their* ideas
"Pseudo" listening, interrupting	"Active" listening
Power tactics/hierarchical	Equal status participants
Discussions at surface level	Diving deep
"Prove" orientation	"Explore" orientation
Mostly make statements	Ask lots of questions
Telling others	Making suggestions
Withholding assumptions	"Stating" assumptions
Seeking to win	Seeking shared understanding
Pushing for closure	Respecting divergent thinking - remaining open-minded

What if They Don't Want to Discuss the Problem At All?

The longer a conflict simmers, the more likely you will see an escalation of emotions. When the conflict catalyst threatens a person's self-worth, the wins and losses become greater for them. Watch for more entrenched win-lose attitudes. When people start to dig in their heels, a mutually agreed solution becomes much harder to achieve.

You may often see finger-pointing and hear words of blame: "They always..." or "They never..." This language ignores the facts and relates only to perceptions. You might see a person avoiding the people with whom they are in conflict. They might even let the other person have their way, just to pretend that the conflict has gone away. Unfortunately, when one person's interests are met at the expense of another's, the root cause has not been identified and addressed. More importantly, the conflict is not likely to go away.

What you can do when you see this happening:

- Speak personally with the person. Seek clarity around the issue and their perceptions of it.

- Remain neutral. Set the tone. Make it safe for them to speak with you about what they're experiencing.

- Keep people focused on the future state. Deep down, they want things to improve. Ask them where they want to be and how they think they can get there.

- Stay focused on objective facts. Make sure that you both have all the relevant details. Clarify assumptions that are misconceptions and generalizations. Push for further understanding of the meaning of their words. For example, "What does…'always' mean?" or "When you call them aggressive, what are you seeing them do? What is their behaviour?"

- Allow adequate time for each person to express their real concerns.

It's possible that, despite your efforts, a person becomes even more strongly tied to their perceptions and beliefs. That's when the conflict tends to become all-consuming. They disengage from solving it and just want to escape from the problem and the people involved. When people expend most of their energy and efforts on a commitment to their own cause, they lose sight of the potential damage their behaviour can cause. When that happens, a team atmosphere can easily become toxic. It becomes quite difficult to get people together for a resolution. Without your intervention, they can remain in this state of discomfort and stress for a long period of time, unable to do anything about it.

What you can do when you see this happening:

- Sift through their emotion to uncover the facts.

- Find out what people are seeing and experiencing. Even though the conflict is an emotional issue, focus on the objective data. Objective and logical reasoning doesn't always persuade people to perceive things differently, but you may at least get agreement on the facts, and facts lead to objective solutions.

COMPETENCY #9: MEDIATE CONFLICTS

- Focus on what the future looks like when the conflict is resolved. Shift their focus to team goals and remind them of how those goals align with what they personally value.

- Recognize that when serious conflicts have escalated, relationships get damaged. It may take time to regenerate those relationships. Sometimes the damage is irreversible in a person's eyes. If that is the case, you may need to help them decide whether staying in their current situation is acceptable.

When all efforts fail, you, as the leader, have the authority to influence the outcome of any conflict resolution process on your team. If you have associates who show little or no willingness to discuss joint interests and continue to push for their individual positions, you need to take a position yourself. Remember, you are a stakeholder. And sometimes, the team needs to see that without a negotiated solution, you will step in to unilaterally determine the best solution for the team. Your position needs to be clearly communicated. It is non-negotiable. The associates must be willing to work together to achieve a mutually agreeable outcome, or they will not work together at all. It's likely that anyone who cannot agree with your imposed decision will either voluntarily leave the team or be asked to go.

Learning Nuggets

This competency is made up of the skills required to mediate interpersonal conflicts on your team.

Remember...

- ✓ View conflict as an opportunity, not a threat.
- ✓ Replace harmful conflict with constructive debate.
- ✓ Address, rather than suppress, conflicts.
- ✓ Seek preventive, not prescriptive, solutions.
- ✓ Ensure people talk *with* each other, not *to* or *at* each other.
- ✓ Guide people toward mutually agreed solutions.

Part Two: Team Leadership Competencies

The complexities of workplace conflict are as diverse as the number of people in an organization. The final Team Leadership competency further explores the important impact of change and transition on individuals and teams. You have gained some insight into ways to manage personal transition and build resilience. Now is the time to provide this valuable insight to your team. Help them reduce stress, build resilience, and prevent potential conflicts during change. That's Competency #10, Lead the People Side of Change.

COMPETENCY #10: LEAD THE PEOPLE SIDE OF CHANGE

"When you lead people through difficult change, you take them on an emotional roller coaster because you are asking them to relinquish something—a belief, a value, a behaviour—that they hold dear. People can stand only so much change at any one time." —Ronald A. Heifetz

In July 2015, McKinsey & Company published the results of a study of hundreds of organizations implementing change initiatives. The study found that as many as 70% of those organizations failed to attain the results they expected. Instead, unintended consequences emerged that tended to involve demoralized and disengaged people. Although the strategies, plans, and processes were well-developed, the outcomes were influenced by one simple truth: change is most likely to be successful when the people who experience it are on board, believe in it, are committed to it, and value it at the personal level. Why do most change programs fail? Mainly, it's due to the fact that people see change as imposed on them. They don't commit because they aren't inspired to do so.

The Myths About Change

If you think like an engineer and believe your organization functions like a machine, then the "fix what's broken" approach is probably your first instinct. The reality is that an organization is a living *system* of people. No problem occurs in isolation. You have to look at the system as a whole entity. You can't compare it to an organization chart that places people into boxes. People don't work in boxes. People work through a network of relationships.

When organizations introduce major change initiatives, four challenges emerge.

1. **Communication:** Communication needs to be front and centre. Your associates need information about what is changing, why it is changing, and how it personally affects them. Without communication, they're left to question where the most trusted sources of information might be.

Part Two: Team Leadership Competencies

2. **Morale and Stress:** Energy levels drop and frustrations mount as associates try to navigate through feelings of instability and personal loss.

3. **Workload and Productivity:** During change, associates may be required to do more with fewer resources. Productivity drops when people feel overwhelmed and unable to meet new demands.

4. **Career Concerns:** Associates know that they could face job losses as a result of mergers, acquisitions, or downsizing initiatives. Competence and employability become major concerns.

Think about some of the past organizational changes you have seen. Which of the four challenges have you personally experienced? Which ones might your associates currently have?

The problems that arise during change are frequently more human than technical. Yet experience shows that organizations spend more time on strategic and tactical issues than they do on the people component of change – it's the one that is most often missed.

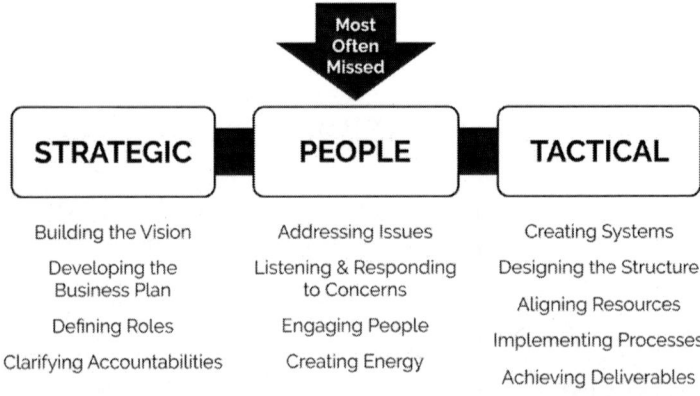

There are always interrelated elements in any change process – the rational (hard) elements that relate to the visible change process and the emotional (soft) elements that represent the invisible and personal transition process. For a change process to succeed, both elements need to be considered. As a team leader, while you must look at change from a strategic and tactical point of view, you need to consider the people side of change too.

COMPETENCY #10: LEAD THE PEOPLE SIDE OF CHANGE

Don't Assume People Know What You Know

Remember that each member of your team has the potential to be a change champion. Don't let them think that you're keeping information from them — they might assume the information you're withholding is bad news. (Otherwise, why would you keep it from them?)

What and *how* you communicate are critical to gaining commitment. When communicating messages during a change, the rule of thumb is to spend more time listening than telling. This means supplementing formal announcements with interpersonal interactions where there is more opportunity to listen than speak. Formal announcements always tell people something. What the teller deems important probably comprises up to 80% of the message. Yet, these messages usually inspire fewer people than expected. This is a problem when you're expecting people to be fully invested in a change. People only commit when they personally deem something important. Leaders often forget this principle when it comes to change communication. They talk about the importance of the change based on what the organization wants, and they forget to address the needs of their audience. It's wise to remember that everyone in the audience first asks themselves, "What's in it for me?"

By nature, your associates are going to be making lots of assumptions. Usually, those assumptions don't serve them, you, or the organization very well. Make sure your associates know everything they need to know to do their jobs. Let them know what's going on and what might be coming down the pike. They can't read your mind, and they may get a lot of false information from other sources. Rumour mills and informal communication channels have a way of taking over and blowing things way out of proportion. Communicate, then communicate even more.

The Link to Intrinsic Drivers

In Part One, we discussed the differences between change and transition. As noted, people look at change from a personal impact point of view. Everyone wants to understand why the change is important. Think about this when you consider the impact of any change on your team. Each person is searching for an answer that connects with what they deem important. If the answer doesn't connect, they are unlikely to support it.

Imagine that you are introducing a new protocol for your team. This protocol will require learning new procedures. Implementing these procedures will be time-consuming, and they will significantly change how the team works together. You talk about the importance of this change in terms of what you believe is its primary benefit. Maybe you stress that the new procedures will allow everyone to know what's happening during each stage of the project. That's the benefit you're selling – but will that benefit resonate for everyone? Are you even aware of the specific issues your associates may be experiencing? Are you able to reference how the new procedures will address their concerns specifically?

Remember that your associates all have different intrinsic drivers. They could all be experiencing different frustrations or wanting different outcomes from the change. Successful change leadership involves getting everyone onside. This is best achieved by helping each person to see the change as addressing something they care about. If there is someone with the Drive for Achievement on the team, they may be frustrated by all the delays that impede completing the project quickly and efficiently. Could there be someone with the Drive for Affiliation? If so, perhaps they are frustrated by low morale or increased stress levels. They could be listening for how these new procedures will alleviate the tensions people are experiencing. And perhaps there's someone with the Drive for Autonomy. Could they be frustrated by the number of team meetings they're now required to attend? They might be looking for a solution that reduces the number of meetings to allow them more time to do their work.

To generate commitment, help your associates perceive the importance of the change from their personal perspective, not from yours. Adapt your communication to align with the varied perspectives of your team. If you don't know how each person perceives the change, the rule of thumb is to consider that your team is made up of a mixture of all three drivers and address each one accordingly.

Build Resilience – *Yours* and *Theirs*

We talked about resilience as a key competency during change (Competency #5). You thought about your own reactions to change. As you know, people feel a loss of personal control when faced with changing roles, responsibilities, procedures, and processes. How each person responds to change reflects their level of resilience. Now you're in a position to lead others through change. How will each associate view the change? Will it make their job easier? Will they have to work harder?

Will their job security be in jeopardy? Will they need to work with different people or learn a new skill?

During change, people become emotional, not rational. Yet leaders tend to sell the change through rational messages, not ones that inspire.

Rational messages talk about change from a fix-what's-not-working angle. In *The Essentials of Appreciative Inquiry*, Bernard Mohr and Jane Watkins reinforce that a focus on "fixing what's wrong" doesn't inspire. And it's not sustainable. Mohr and Watkins believe that what works better is a more positive, forward-looking approach, one that's based on shifting a person's perceptions. Your job as a team leader is to allow someone to see something better. Help them imagine experiencing something different or creating something new – something they can believe in. Beliefs are powerful drivers of behaviour. When someone believes something to be true or inspiring, it generates an energy that empowers them to move forward.

So, as you help people build the required technical skills associated with a change, you also need to address the underlying beliefs that enable people to use their skills to their fullest. Ignoring the intrinsic drivers of your associates during a change initiative runs the risk of addressing only the symptoms of the problems that arise, not the root causes. Investigate why people respond in unexpected ways. Delve into the root causes and gain insight into what inspires someone to move forward in a positive way.

Lead People Through Transition

Your insight into what drives people helps you understand how people are feeling and what you can do to guide them through their transition process.

To do this, start with your own self-insight. Remember the Scott and Jaffe transition model presented in Competency #5. This model is your reference for leading others through change. Review the insights you gained. First, understand how you're dealing with the change at your own personal level. Identify where *you* are in your transition process. Be especially aware of the impact of your behaviour and words if you are in Resistance. Focus on what you personally need in order to have the positive energy that's required to help others. You must lead yourself before you lead others.

Part Two: Team Leadership Competencies

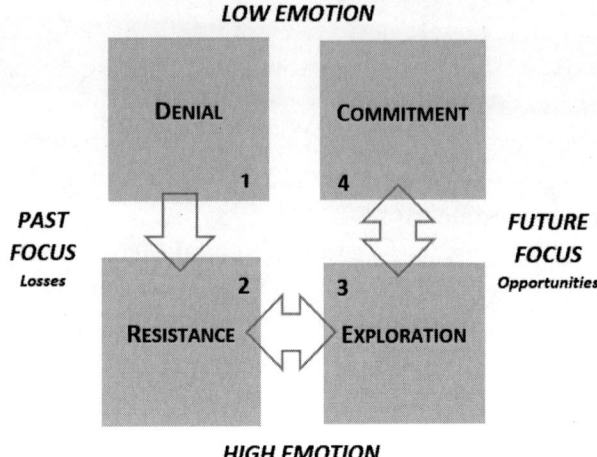

Don't Assume Your Associates Are Where You Are

As a team leader, you know what's coming sooner than your associates do. You have more time for the impact of a change to sink in. By the time you present the change to your team, you've travelled along your own personal journey of transition and may already have arrived on the right side of the transition curve, looking at the opportunities. It's highly unlikely that your associates are there with you.

William Bridges, author of the book *Managing Transitions*, refers to the importance of what he termed the Marathon Effect. He describes how, in a marathon, the front runners are often well into the race before the last runners have even started. As a front runner, you are in a different place. Don't forget that your associates aren't with you at the front. They're at the back. This is especially relevant when major change initiatives have taken many months of preparation before implementation. The senior leaders move through the initial months of planning while their subordinates remain unaware that a change is even coming. Once it's announced, the leaders expect everyone to just get on board. But as the following image shows, the others need time to catch up.

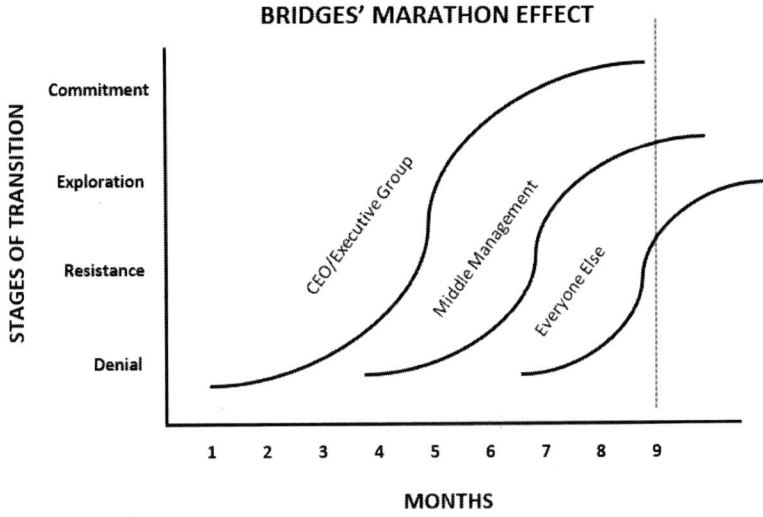

To understand the mindset of others, consider how long it took for you to adjust to the news and cope with your feelings about the change. As with a marathon, everyone arrives at the destination at different times. Appreciate where your associates are on their personal transition curve. Don't push them – pull them along. Give them the time and resources they personally need to arrive there under their own energy and initiative. Engage in discussions about the change and let them know that you are open to listening to their concerns. Solicit their questions. Answer those that you can. And engage them as much as possible in the change process.

Understand What They Need and Want

When it comes to understanding what people want during change, American journalist Sydney J. Harris put it aptly when he said, "our dilemma is that we hate change and love it at the same time; what we really want is for things to remain the same but get better." People don't usually seek change until the pain of not changing exceeds the pain of changing. This is true even if they recognize that changes are needed. After being in a job for a while, people grow comfortable doing things a certain way – even if they don't like how things are done.

Remember the needs people have at each stage of transition. Different needs require different leadership responses. Review the needs and responses below, and keep them in mind as you lead your team through change:

Denial – *Provide accurate information.* You need to ensure that each associate understands what's changing and why. Where possible, answer the what, when, where, how, and why questions of the change. Provide as much information as you can to make the outcomes of the change personally relevant to the individual who's in Denial.

Resistance – *Be responsive to the associate's needs.* Provide social support, a safe place to vent, and the opportunity to problem-solve. Remember the importance of *asking*, not *telling*. Listen for understanding and ask, "How can I help?" That one question is immensely powerful in this stage.

Exploration – *Now is the time to empower.* Provide encouragement, advice, and focus; capitalize on the team member's renewed energy; and provide opportunities for new learning. Find ways to maximize their intrinsic strengths with tasks that achieve valued outcomes.

Commitment – *Reinforce and reward performance.* Support the associate's ideas; reinforce their value and recognize their contributions in meaningful ways.

More About Resistance – Because It's Important!

During any change process, it is normal for people to resist. This chart illustrates resistance along a scale, and as you can see, up to 80% can fall somewhere between active resistance and neutral.

COMPETENCY #10: LEAD THE PEOPLE SIDE OF CHANGE

THE RESISTANCE SPECTRUM

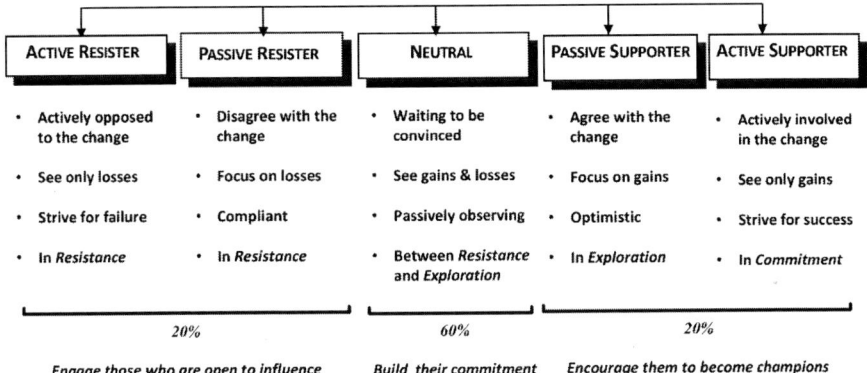

Your challenge is to positively influence the passive resisters, who exhibit opposition to some degree, and those who are neutral, just waiting to be convinced. Those who you identify as active supporters have the potential to champion the change process. They are the best people to positively influence their peers.

Active resisters are immune to any attempt to influence their way of looking at things. So consider the time and effort you would need to expend in your attempt to shift their perspective. It's true that most people first focus on what's wrong with a change rather than what's right, and that over time, many are often willing to shift their thinking. However, there are always a few people who, no matter what efforts you make, refuse to see things differently. Spend your energy on those associates who you feel you can have an impact on. They are the ones who make a difference.

By the way, as I've mentioned before, don't confuse commitment with compliance. There's a big difference between the two. A compliant person is likely still in Resistance. They may appear committed, when in fact, they are compliant. You often are able to see non-compliant behaviour, but compliant behaviour is harder to detect. That's because compliance looks much like commitment. But it isn't commitment. A compliant person goes through the motions of doing as they are told, not because they want to, but because they believe they must. Their discretionary effort is minimal – just enough to get by. Unfortunately, they're actually not onside. Take the time to learn whether your associates are committed or compliant.

Part Two: Team Leadership Competencies

There are specific reasons why people resist change. Your responses can make a difference. Here are some of the most common reasons that people resist change, and suggestions for addressing their concerns:

Fear of the unknown – Uncertainty and anxiety stems from not knowing the future state. You can help your associate see a more positive future by articulating the vision and connecting it to what they value.

Fear of failure – Some associates may be concerned that the required skills are beyond their capabilities. Express confidence in them and support their continuous learning.

Not understanding the *why* of the change – Sometimes, the logical reason for a change doesn't resonate with an associate. Communicate the need for it in a way they can understand from their own perspective – not just yours. Address their WIIFM question.

Disagreement with the need for the change – When an associate can't see the rationale for the change, they won't buy into it. Listen and acknowledge their point of view. This builds a foundation of trust. Let them know their perspective matters. They don't need to be convinced that they're wrong; they just need to support a decision that has already been made.

A Sense of Loss – Your associates may be feeling that they're losing something they value. Acknowledge these feelings. Don't try to persuade them that what they're feeling is ridiculous. Try to determine what they perceive they are losing. Could it be money, power, colleagues, job security? Shift their focus to potential gains consistent with their intrinsic driver.

Inertia, fatigue, and burn-out – During change, people are often too tired to put in the required effort. Remember, the energy you bring to work influences the energy of others. They are looking at you for inspiration. Energy is contagious.

COMPETENCY #10: LEAD THE PEOPLE SIDE OF CHANGE

The best way to help your associates become more comfortable, satisfied, committed, and engaged with a change is to understand their driver. What do they care most about? What are their concerns? What questions do they need to have answered? And answer those questions in a timely manner.

For someone with the Drive for Achievement, their questions might include:

- What will be the outcome of this change?
- What are the opportunities?
- Will it get done, and by when?
- Who's leading the process and making the key decisions?
- What resources will be required – people, financial, technical?
- What's going to stand in our way and slow us down?
- Who will keep us on track?
- How will I be rewarded for my contributions?
- Will I be financially rewarded when I do more with less?
- How will this benefit my career growth?
- Will I be given more responsibility or authority?

For someone with the Drive for Affiliation, their questions might include:

- Who's going to be impacted by this change?
- Are we being told the truth?
- How will my colleagues be treated?
- Will my work relationships change?
- Will I be included in or excluded from decisions that affect me?
- Does management care about us?
- How will this affect the culture of our team/our organization?
- Will I be acknowledged for any of my contributions?
- Will I be given more work with less support?
- Will people be let go?
- How will this affect me personally?

For someone with the Drive for Autonomy, their questions might include:

- How does this change make sense?
- Why are decisions being made so quickly, without due diligence?
- Has management assessed all the risks?
- Where's the supporting data?
- Are we managing risk?
- Haven't we learned from past mistakes?
- Will processes change?
- Who will ensure changes are implemented the right way?
- What will I learn?
- How can I contribute my knowledge and expertise?
- How will we measure the outcomes?

People Commit When They're Inspired

Suppose your team needs to adapt to new technology. Before thinking that people are resistant to the change, ask first how the technology might make it easier for them to do the work they value doing. Once you form the link between their purpose and the tools, they are more likely to be willing to learn new ways of doing things.

Your associates need to have information to decide whether a change is desirable. They're not likely to embrace a change because you tell them to. They'll commit when inspired. They need to understand the why of the change from their own perspective. Be open to listening and acknowledge their point of view. If you want to pull people along, allow them to see that what they do is meaningful and valued. Then watch the energy when someone lights up and takes notice.

Learning Nuggets

This competency is made up of the skills required to lead your team members through organizational change.

Remember...

- ✓ People trust behaviour more than words – your behaviours should mirror what you say.
- ✓ The head is more important than the heart – understanding comes before commitment.
- ✓ Listening outweighs telling when you need to get people onside.
- ✓ People can handle the truth – what they can't handle are uncertainty and mistrust.
- ✓ People complain before they move on – it's human nature to "moan and groan our way to action."

This completes the five Team Leadership competencies. You are now ready to move to the third set of competencies that focus on generating corporate energy.

ORGANIZATIONAL LEADERSHIP COMPETENCIES

Generate Corporate Energy

"Strategic leaders must not get consumed by the operational and tactical side of their work. They have a duty to find time to shape the future."
—Stephanie S. Mead

Organizational Leadership

- 12. TRANSFORM CULTURE
- 11. INSPIRE PURPOSE, VISION & VALUES
- **GENERATE CORPORATE ENERGY**

Team Leadership

- 10. LEAD THE PEOPLE SIDE OF CHANGE
- 9. MEDIATE CONFLICTS
- 8. BUILD COHESIVE TEAMS
- 7. COACH FOR ACUITY
- 6. FACILITATE PERFORMANCE POTENTIAL
- ACHIEVE RESULTS THROUGH OTHERS

Personal Leadership

- 5. BUILD RESILIENCE
- 4. PREVENT, MANAGE & RESOLVE CONFLICT
- 3. COMMUNICATE WITH INFLUENCE
- 2. BALANCE INTRINSIC STRENGTHS
- 1. ACQUIRE INSIGHT INTO SELF AND OTHERS
- DEVELOP PERSONAL & INTERPERSONAL EFFECTIVENESS

Part Two: Organizational Leadership Competencies

Organizational Leaders Generate Corporate Energy

"Employees at every level, at every location and in every division have a part to play. It springs from something deep inside people that makes them want to work enthusiastically, with their hearts and heads as well as their hands. Corporate energy drives employee commitment to superb service and when necessary, empowers them to change the course of events for the better." —Art McNeil

We have looked at leadership from both personal and team perspectives. You have arrived at the top tier of your organization and you are now required to lead the enterprise. The Personal and Team Leadership competencies you have reviewed up to this point will serve you well in this senior executive role – along with two additional ones that are specifically required to generate energy in your organization. Now you're going to take an organizational perspective and look at how it all fits together.

Energy Fuels Productivity

The most valuable resource of an organization is the energy that is waiting to be tapped. Yet, it seems that many organizations suffer from an energy crisis. Management practices, while essential, often destroy the energy throughout the organization. An imbalanced focus on systems, practices, policies, and procedures has a way of draining passion and enthusiasm. In his book, *The "I" of the Hurricane*, Art McNeil talks about the fact that organizations have spent years "training leadership out of people...In a policy-driven culture, people spend a lot of energy watching their backs and making sure nothing goes wrong."

Consider how your organization appears to someone who walks in the front door of your business. What might they see? Do they see a sense of vitality and energy, or do they see people dragging themselves in, coffee in hand, looking tired and stressed? What do *you* see? Do people seem more excited when they leave the building on Friday afternoons or when they come in on Monday mornings – do your employees demonstrate a TGIF or TGIM mentality?

Personal Purpose + Culture Fit = Energy

In a 2018 Harvard Business Review article titled "The Culture Factor," authors Boris Groysberg, Jeremiah Lee, Jesse Price, and J. Yo-Jud Cheng wrote: "Culture can unleash tremendous amounts of energy toward a shared purpose and foster an organization's capacity to thrive. Culture is a group phenomenon. It cannot exist solely within a single person, nor is it simply the average of individual characteristics. It resides in shared behaviours, values, and assumptions and is most commonly experienced through the norms and expectations of a group – that is, the unwritten rules."

Cultural norms define what is encouraged, discouraged, accepted, or rejected within an organization. When these are aligned with each person's intrinsic driver, they can generate collective energy. For example...

- A person with the Drive for Achievement might be more energized in a culture that focuses on *results.* A results-oriented culture is characterized by a shared drive for goal attainment. These are work environments where intrinsic strengths such as competitiveness, decisiveness, boldness, and risk-taking are valued.

- A person with a Drive for Affiliation might be more energized in a culture that focuses on *service.* A service-oriented culture is characterized by a shared drive for collaborative relationships. These are work environments where intrinsic strengths such as loyalty, altruism, sincerity, and compassion are valued.

- A person with a Drive for Autonomy might be more energized in a culture that focuses on *procedure.* A procedure-oriented culture is characterized by thoughtful planning and order. These are work environments where intrinsic strengths such as analysis, caution, thoroughness, and self-reliance are valued.

However, it's important to note that healthy organizational cultures create opportunities for *all* employees to achieve a sense of self-worth, regardless of their driver. Some people naturally align with an organization's culture, while others are encouraged to recognize how their driver can add value to that culture.

Part Two: Organizational Leadership Competencies

You Have the Power to Generate Energy

Outstanding executive teams are those that demonstrate Relationship Acuity. Your organization's potential depends upon the *collective* quality of your leadership team. Does your team function as an interrelated group of strategic leaders with a collaborative focus on building the performance of your organization? Executive behaviours and attitudes inevitably get replicated down through the organization. If the senior team is cohesive, aligned, and engaged, it is likely that other teams are too. The result is an *energy-efficient* organization. If your team doesn't demonstrate those qualities, you run the risk of creating an energy-*deficient* organization.

Energy Efficiency Requires Cohesion, Engagement, and Alignment – At All Levels

Leadership teams frequently experience issues related to cohesion, engagement, and alignment. Without cohesion, there is no shared sense of purpose; without alignment, there is no shared vision; without engagement, there are no shared values. Without those things, everyone is just doing their job. All three interrelated components are the primary source of energy in your organization. There are three primary indicators of an energy-efficient organization:

1. **Inclusive relationships** – there is *cohesion* between people and on teams

2. **High-performing people** – there is *engagement* at all levels

3. **An integrated culture** – there is *alignment* to the organization's purpose, vision, and values

Before reviewing the two Organizational Leadership competencies, first look at yourself as an organizational leader. Then, take a close look at your team.

Self-Analysis

How Do You See Yourself as an Organizational Leader?
This is your validation. Place a check mark beside the phrases that apply to you. What are your blind spots?

- ☐ My sense of purpose is infused in everything I do and say
- ☐ I am aware of the impact of my behaviour in my interactions with my fellow team members
- ☐ I show, by example, commitment to my continuous development as a leader
- ☐ I acknowledge the importance of interpersonal relationships on our team
- ☐ I recognize the importance of teamwork for the success of our team and our organization
- ☐ I see the significance of integrating a strong sense of purpose on our team
- ☐ I think about ways to create a positive work environment for all employees across the organization
- ☐ I focus on how our organization can become one of the best places to work

How Do You See Your Team as a Group of Organizational Leaders?
The following are some symptoms of a leadership team that lacks cohesion, engagement, or alignment. Do you see any of these symptoms on your team?

- ☐ Inattention in meetings – reading, writing, e-mails, checking phone messages, taking phone calls
- ☐ Working as a "reporting" group, not an "interactive" team
- ☐ Long "silo" briefings from each function head, after which no one comments
- ☐ Members work in isolation as independent function heads, not interdependent leaders
- ☐ Discussions stay tactical, in the weeds; strategic issues are rarely addressed
- ☐ No one asks challenging questions
- ☐ Energy is low; stress and frustration are visible

Part Two: Organizational Leadership Competencies

Team dysfunction often boils down to a siloed versus interdependent team model. When a team functions in silos, team members don't often operate as an interconnected unit with a shared vision and purpose; instead, each team member is focused on their own functional area of responsibility.

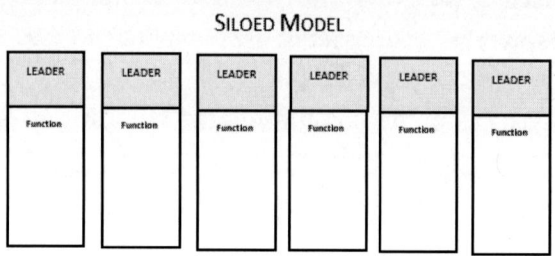

By contrast, on an interdependent leadership team, leaders each manage their functional areas and, at the same time, work collaboratively in service of the stakeholders of the organization.

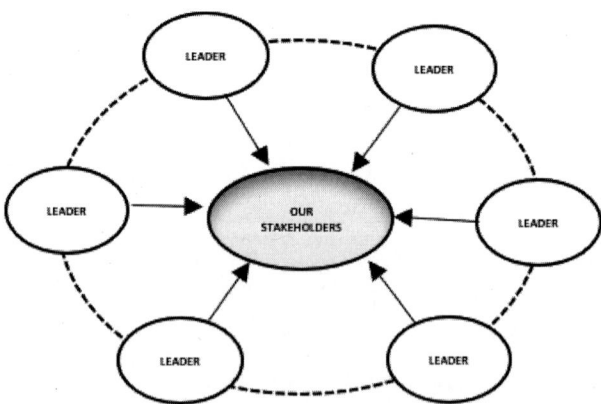

Team Analysis

Think about your experiences and the behaviours you and your fellow executives demonstrate on a day-to-day basis. Place a check mark in the box that you believe is most appropriate. All team members could participate in this exercise, which would make for an interesting discussion.

Generate Corporate Energy

We as a Team...	Almost Never	On Occasion	Almost Always
1. Focus on integrating a strong sense of purpose across our organization			
2. Create, communicate, and foster a vision of what can be achieved			
3. Demonstrate organizational values in our day-to-day behaviours and lead by example			
4. Ensure all employees are aligned with our organizational purpose, vision, and values			
5. Operate with a sense of unity around everything we do			
6. Challenge each other to think systemically			
7. Focus on our teamwork and respect each person's point of view			
8. Focus on issues, not personalities			
9. Table conflict openly with constructive debate			
10. See diversity as a strategic advantage			
11. Appreciate and make use of each person's intrinsic strengths			
12. Acknowledge the value of work relationships across our organization			

Pay attention to those items marked *Almost Never*. After reviewing competencies #11 and #12, consider ways that the team could move those check marks to the right.

COMPETENCY #11: Inspire Purpose, Vision, and Values

> *"An organization's success has more to do with clarity of shared purpose, common principles, and strength of belief in them than to assets, expertise, operating ability, or management competence, important as they may be."*
> —Dee Hock

Together, purpose, vision, and values provide direction for everything people do in an organization and how they're expected to do it. They are interrelated and cross every level of leadership, from individual contributors to enterprise-wide leaders. At the organizational level, purpose, vision, and values define *why* the organization exists, *where* it needs to go, and *how* it wants to get there. Together, these three elements provide direction for everything that happens in an organization. At the team level, each team has a defined purpose, a vision, and values. At the personal level, each individual has their own sense of purpose – the driver that defines *why* they do what they do. Individual purpose generates a vision of *where* a person wants to go, and their values drive their behaviours – *how* they want to get there.

COMPETENCY #11: Inspire Purpose, Vision, and Values

Your organization's purpose defines its differentiation within your industry. Your vision is the desired picture of your organization in the future. Your values define how people are expected to behave to fulfill your organization's purpose and vision – how they get things done. Values and behaviours, together, drive the practices that define your organization's culture.

When you inspire purpose, vision, and values, you are getting people to *want to* belong to something bigger than themselves.

Your challenge is to create a stimulating and challenging work environment for everyone. It's not easy to energize employees who differ with regard to what they care about. But it's important to work hard at it. Create energy in people, and you won't need to push them. Their energy will pull them toward their goals. You know when your organization is having an energy crisis when you see low discretionary effort and mediocre performance across your organization. Ask yourself, "how well do our employees understand the connection between their role and our organization's sense of purpose? In what way do they perceive that they're contributing to making our vision of the future a reality? Do they feel a sense of personal pride and engagement in helping to drive our business forward?"

An Organization's Mission Is Its Purpose

Energy comes from a collective purpose or reason for being. Your organization's purpose is articulated through your mission statement. Make it meaningful. Without a clear and consistent mission statement, teams are likely to develop their own unique cultures. It is common to see conflicts between sales and operations, HR and finance, or marketing and R&D, because each unit develops its own set of values and its own culture. It's easy to see how these cultural differences can fragment an organization and lead to non-productive conflict. What's needed is a mission statement that binds all functions within your organization together.

Inspire to Engage

Organizations have vast reservoirs of energy just waiting to be released. And that energy is released when people are inspired. Deep inside us all, there's a desire for inspiration. People want to feel passion, enthusiasm, and commitment to their work. No one wants to do a bad job. But it's hard to do a good job when you've become disengaged.

Part Two: Organizational Leadership Competencies

People have a huge amount of energy that they can apply as discretionary effort – that's what differentiates average performance from exceptional. Inspired people get a lot done for your business. Uninspired people don't.

You can visually identify people who are engaged in their work. They seek challenges. They work harder yet show less stress than others. At the same time, you can visually identify people who are *disengaged* because they are merely compliant. They do as much as is required, and no more. They become the so-called "deadwood" of an organization. When your people are disengaged, organizational performance suffers.

Sometimes your star performers become disengaged employees, and then they leave. Departures are sometimes prompted by a call from an external recruiter, or by a desire for more money or a better work location, but often star performers leave in search of a more inspiring work environment. If your organization is losing good people, your team needs to look for the reasons why. What is it that your organization doesn't offer? What do people need? Every senior leader should realize that part of their job is to ensure that their best people stay.

The Perception Connection

In the early 1980s, work environments offered job security and competitive salaries. The next twenty years, however, brought recessions that led to rightsizing, reengineering, and downsizing initiatives. People lost faith in their employers. Trust plummeted. People were gripped by the fear of losing their jobs. The outplacement business was booming. Consultants walked into client organizations for the express purpose of walking people out, many of whom didn't see it coming. Many wondered why they were chosen to go while some of their colleagues got to stay. Hostile survivors, who got to stay but would have preferred to leave, were sent to transition workshops. Fractured relationships between employees and management generated an *'us versus them'* mentality. The perception was "management doesn't care."

Today, employee expectations have changed. People no longer expect lifetime employment with one company. The new perception is to "take care of yourself because no one else will." Organizations have to fight for the best people, and they work hard to become "employers of choice." Employees want to know: "What's the company's reputation? What is its value proposition? Does it offer a rewarding environment? Is it a place I want to work? Is it a place to grow my career?"

COMPETENCY #11: INSPIRE PURPOSE, VISION, AND VALUES

People also want to see that what they are doing is, in some way, worthwhile. This is more difficult today, at a time when the focus in our world seems to have moved from quality to quantity. Author Warren Bennis talks about how quality connects intimately to our perceptions of meaning and value in our lives. As he puts it, "When we love our work, we need not be managed by hopes of reward or fears of punishment. We can create systems that facilitate our work, rather than being preoccupied with checks and controls of people who want to beat or exploit the system."

Every job is necessary, or it wouldn't exist in the first place. One of the best perks you can offer is the perception of purpose and value in a person's job. In essence, create a *line of sight* to a meaningful collective goal. Let it be seen as valuable. Elevate the stature of even the most mundane role. Get people to believe they are building something grand, not just laying the bricks.

A Vision Inspires

Organizational energy comes from a shared vision that inspires. A vision is a mental picture of a preferred future state that people can buy into. There's an old saying: "If you don't know where you're going, how will you know you've arrived?" By the same token, you can't lead people if they don't know where they are going. Hopefully, it's someplace inspiring. Dr. Martin Luther King Jr. said, "I have a dream." He didn't say, "I have an objective." His dream was a desired future state of racial equality.

Your vision is the picture of where you're going. A vision gives people a sense of direction. It's not just goals and objectives. It's a preferred future state. A vision can be presented through meaningful metaphors that describe how your customers, shareholders, and employees see you in the future.

Each employee looks at your vision through their own lens, of course. When they hear or read about it, they look for a match with their own vision for success and their own drive for self-worth. When you communicate your vision, consider whether it's inspiring. Does it encourage people to *come along* with you – to see what you see?

Words alone don't create a common picture. We know that people listen with their own personal perception. And what they see is more powerful than what they hear. When you hear something, you create your own vision of what it looks like, just like when you're reading a book. How often have people said that movies based on books don't live up to the images they had in their minds? That's because they had created their own vision of what the characters and scenes looked like to them.

Ask each member of your team to imagine being in a helicopter flying over the organization five years into the future. What do they each see? Why is it important to them? This exercise provides meaning and value to your operational goals and objectives. Remember, everyone sees a vision from their own personal perspective, based on what they value. Have each of your colleagues share their responses. Expect different perspectives. Diversity is healthy. It ultimately leads to increased clarity, understanding, and mutual agreement.

Values Drive Behaviours

Values are intrinsic to a person, a team, and an organization, because they represent what the person, team, or organization believes in. People interpret values differently. When people visibly see a value in action the way they interpret it, they believe in it. When they don't, they lose faith in the integrity of their organization. Each person is looking for evidence of stated values in the day-to-day behaviours of their senior leaders. They judge what they see based on their individual interpretations of each value. They have expectations of their colleagues and their leaders, and when those expectations fall short, they're likely to grow disengaged.

Writer Patrick Lencioni, in an HBR article titled "Make Your Values Mean Something," wrote: "Consider the motherhood-and-apple-pie values that appear in so many companies' values statements – integrity, teamwork, ethics, quality, customer satisfaction, and innovation. In fact, 55% of all Fortune 100 companies claim integrity is a core value, 49% espouse customer satisfaction, and 40% tout teamwork. While these are inarguably good qualities, such terms hardly provide a distinct blueprint for employee behaviour. Cookie-cutter values don't set a company apart from competitors; they make it fade into the crowd."

Lencioni further asks, "What's the first thing many executives do after they decide to embark on a values initiative? They hand off the effort to the HR department, which uses the initiative as an excuse for an inclusive feel-good effort. To engage employees, HR rolls out employee surveys and holds lots of town meetings to gather input and build consensus.... Values initiatives have nothing to do with building consensus – they're about imposing a set of fundamental, strategically sound beliefs on a broad group of people."

Don't Let Your Values Become Doorstops

The executives in one of my client organizations had actual paperweights engraved with their corporate values. When I asked one manager to speak to his organization's values, he pointed to the floor where his paperweight was holding his door open and said, "I found a good use for them." In that organization, it seemed that the managers didn't pay much attention to the words, nor did they remember any of them.

Values are more than what's posted on the office walls. Values define how people are expected to behave and how they are treated. They form the culture of an organization – the way the work gets done. Unfortunately, most value statements are often uninspiring. They're just seen as words on a page, and they're poor descriptors of what really happens in your organization. Your challenge is to make your values meaningful. Remember that people perceive values through their own personal lens. Consider different intrinsic drivers when you communicate. This ensures that people driven by different things see the value from their perspective, not just yours.

It is incumbent on your leadership team to draft your value statements with sincerity and authenticity. People notice when there's an honest attempt to show what differentiates your organization from others. Be specific about what each value means. Go beyond broad statements and clarify guiding principles to describe and define expected behaviours.

When your team develops your values statements, check for individual perceptions of those values among your colleagues, and ask them each to translate the values into concrete actions. This is more difficult than it appears. Your team leaders may say they understand and embrace the values, but then have difficulty describing the behaviour that would visually demonstrate each value day-to-day. Remember, words mean different things to different people. And different meanings lead to different behaviours.

I was once involved in the merger of two large organizations with very different cultures. One company focused on marketing and innovation, the other on financial strength. A struggle ensued on the new

Part Two: Organizational Leadership Competencies

executive team. It had fourteen members made up of senior leaders from each organization, and two of the most senior leaders became known as the two fighting heads. Each brought their own beliefs and values to the table, and because there were two factions, the team struggled to become a cohesive whole.

The group did manage to agree on the values that represented their newly merged organization: *integrity, trust, accountability,* and *collaboration*. I divided the leaders into three random groups and asked each group to rank the values in order of importance and to define the behaviours that would demonstrate each. They really struggled with it! Differences in intrinsic drivers surfaced. It became clear that each person's driver influenced their expectations for how a value should be demonstrated. While to one person, trust meant honest communication, another interpreted it to mean following corporate policies and procedures. Another saw trust to mean effective and timely communication of information.

Of course, there were no right or wrong answers. The importance of this exercise was to show them that they had different perspectives on each value and its meaning.

Having observed your colleagues over a period of time, you may have noticed different perspectives around your executive table. When there are different perspectives, you can bet that interpretations of value words and statements also differ. That's why asking questions about what matters most to each team member can make the difference between a mediocre values exercise and a more effective one. For example, ask each leader: "What does each value mean to you?" "Why is it important?" "In what order would you rank these values in terms of their significance to our organization?" and "How do you plan to demonstrate this value every day? What will people in our organization see you doing?" These questions are not easy to answer, so when I pose these questions to executive teams, many interpretations surface. As you expose and discuss everyone's different viewpoints, you are much more likely to find some alignment, preventing the inevitable conflicts that occur when expectations are assumed but never clarified.

COMPETENCY #11: INSPIRE PURPOSE, VISION, AND VALUES

The Meaning of Values

People buy into values that are meaningful to them. This means they interpret value words based on their own intrinsic driver. Consider how the meaning of three sample values can differ, depending on the person interpreting it:

Honesty:

- Achievement Driver – to do what you say you're going to do
- Affiliation Driver – to be truthful, without an agenda
- Autonomy Driver – to share the appropriate and correct information

Integrity:

- Achievement Driver – to get it done
- Affiliation Driver – to build trust
- Autonomy Driver – to hold to a principle

Commitment:

- Achievement Driver – to deliver on goals
- Affiliation Driver – to meet the needs of others
- Autonomy Driver – to ensure things are done well

Engage your team in a discussion about how people read words differently. No one's meaning of a value is the right one. What's most important is consistency within an organization.

To ensure consistency, suggest that your team engage in a process to reach an agreement on the *meaning* of each of your values and *clarify* the specific observable behaviours expected of each one. This may take time, but it's well worth it in the long run.

Here are two examples of how a team might define values and clarify the associated behaviours.

Part Two: Organizational Leadership Competencies

VALUE: PEOPLE

Meaning: Our most valued resources are our employees and our partners in business – our customers and suppliers.

Clarification: We demonstrate this value when we...
- ✓ listen to and understand the views of others
- ✓ involve others in decisions that will directly affect them
- ✓ recognize and respect individual differences
- ✓ demonstrate a positive attitude to our work and our colleagues
- ✓ align individual goals with corporate goals
- ✓ cultivate the future leadership of the organization

VALUE: INITIATIVE

Meaning: We exceed our customers' expectations by providing insights, products, and services that add value to their operations.

Clarification: We demonstrate this value when we...
- ✓ are not afraid of making tough decisions
- ✓ finish what we start
- ✓ act decisively
- ✓ focus on achieving results
- ✓ share information in a timely way
- ✓ anticipate and prevent problems before they occur

You Are the Ultimate Role Model

Remember the adage *seeing is believing*. It's never been *hearing is believing*. Behaviour overrides words. When it comes to getting people to believe in something, the words you say aren't as important as the behaviour you exhibit. People believe what they see. It's their perception of "what's really going on around here."

Every action you take, every behaviour people see, sends a message. It's a way of communicating your values. As you can guess, problems emerge when verbal and non-verbal messages conflict. When the verbal message is "we put our people first," but the behaviour shows that cost-cutting matters more, people don't believe the words. And the perception of these non-verbal signals can travel through a rumour mill that takes on a life of its own.

Here's a great example of such conflicting messages. During a period of austerity, the senior management team of a national hotel organization I worked with decided to reduce budgets and cancel the Christmas gift packages that, in previous years, had been handed out to all employees. The message was that there was a need for fiscal restraint. The staff might have believed the importance of this message had they not perceived contrary behaviour. Over the holiday season, the executives travelled to meet with the management teams of their hotels. The morning after each overnight stay, the room attendants found empty champagne bottles in the rooms. When I asked one senior leader why his team chose to behave in such a contrary way during a time of restraint, he said that they deserved the reward for all their hard work that year!

This leads me to the concept of *CEO Disease*. Psychologist and author Tasha Eurich coined this term to describe the ignorance executives often have about how others perceive them. The higher up the ladder they climb, the less likely they are to receive honest feedback, and the less self-aware they become. Reflect on whether this is true for you. If you have CEO Disease, you need to re-focus on your self-insight, your self-management, and your Relationship Acuity. It's time to clearly see the impact of your words and behaviours on others. Focus on generating the energy that comes from positive perspectives throughout the organization.

Actions Speak Louder Than Words

Your actions need to be consistent with the values of your organization. That's the only way people will perceive senior executives to be trustworthy and authentic. Your performance, your conversations, and your actions demonstrate the values that you believe are important to the organization. Your visible behaviour demonstrates what you believe in.

Putting thoughts and beliefs into action is difficult. Coming up with the right actions at the right time, given the situation and the people involved in each instance, is even more difficult. Focus on how you can ignite energy in each person with whom you interact. How can you articulate and embody your organization's values?

Part Two: Organizational Leadership Competencies

The minute you make the decision that you want to know how others perceive you, you've increased your self-insight. You can't acquire more effective styles of relating without the help of others. Gather feedback from as many people in your sphere of influence as you can, up, down, and across the organization. They see you much more objectively than you do. Gathering feedback from your peers around the executive table, as well as your direct reports, is like mining for gold. Ask them point-blank: How do they perceive you? How well do you listen to them? How open are you to their different perspectives?

Focus on your strengths, and consider which ones are overused, underused, and misapplied. Then practice applying new behaviours until they require less forethought and are perceived by you and others as authentic. Mental rehearsals are powerful. Visualize ways to handle anticipated interactions. Ask questions, and listen before you respond. Anticipate your automatic responses, then imagine responding differently. Experiment with new behaviours. Eventually, you'll move from awareness through to *conscious* competence. When that happens, a genuine change will have occurred.

Look in Before You Look Out

As a starting point, your leadership team needs to look inward to discover each team member's intrinsic driver and intrinsic strengths. Then look outward, not just to your systems and processes but also to your employees. They truly are your most valuable resource.

Looking in: You already know that different people view things differently, based on what they care about. As an organizational leader, understanding these differing perceptions is critical. Around the table, recognize that each of your colleagues views a situation in their own unique way. Everyone needs to hear and understand the varied perspectives in order to move toward problem-solving.

Power plays a significant role at the executive table. Based on the concepts in this book, you now know some of the best synonyms for power are energy, drive, and influence. The real sources of power at the organizational leadership level exist *intrinsically* within each leader. Tapping into it requires that each leader have self-insight – know their intrinsic strengths, be fully engaged, and experience a sense of fulfillment in their work. Without that self-awareness, the source of power

COMPETENCY #11: INSPIRE PURPOSE, VISION, AND VALUES

becomes extrinsic. You can see evidence of extrinsic power in the senior leaders who try to control others.

When engaged in developing your mission statement, consider the importance of words and messages that inspire. Encourage the team to focus on its diverse viewpoints about the organization's purpose. Ask them to think about their responses to the following questions: "Why do we exist? What is our basic purpose? What is unique or distinctive about us?" Responses to these questions surface individual perspectives and provide the opportunity for the team to see and appreciate different points of view. Once individual perspectives are tabled, reach agreement on the key messages your mission should include and address how you demonstrate this sense of purpose through your actions. What will people perceive regarding the way you deliver your business results? How will you go about fulfilling your mission?

Looking out: The most important relationships in your organization are between team leaders and their associates. As the most senior team leaders, your role is to ensure that your direct reports are aware of *their* role in inspiring and engaging *their* associates. Consider the five Team Leadership competencies in terms of how they are demonstrated by the people who report to you.

Place a check mark beside those questions to which you would answer *yes*.

- ☐ Do your team leaders respect each of their associates, and do they understand why each role matters?
- ☐ Do they reinforce the importance of each of their associates' roles?
- ☐ Do they invest time in getting to know their associates personally so they can partner with them for their growth and development?
- ☐ Do they engage one-on-one with their associates, ask for input, and listen for understanding?
- ☐ Do they value different perspectives and engage in meaningful dialogue?
- ☐ Do they provide constant, consistent, and meaningful feedback so that their associates are energized, not exhausted?

Part Two: Organizational Leadership Competencies

☐ Do they enable their associates to see the direct connection between what they do and the organization's purpose, vision, and values?

Where there are missing check marks, focus on increasing their competence as team leaders. After all, you can't inspire purpose, vision, and values throughout your organization without them.

Learning Nuggets

This competency is made up of the skills required to inspire people at all levels of your organization.

Remember...

✓ Organizational energy comes from a collective purpose and a vision that inspires.

✓ The best perk you can offer an employee is the perception of purpose and value in their work.

✓ Values drive behaviours – so be sure to clarify the meaning of your values in visible terms.

✓ Ensure the people who report to you understand how to inspire and engage the people that report to them.

✓ If your organization is losing good people, look for the reasons why.

You create your organization's unique culture when you inspire purpose, vision, and values across the enterprise. Continually take the pulse of your organization to ensure its ongoing health and well-being. When symptoms of culture-distress occur, be vigilant and proactive. And this leads us to Competency #12, Transform Culture.

COMPETENCY #12: Transform Culture

> *"Culture does not change because we desire to change it. Culture changes when the organization is transformed – the culture reflects the realities of people working together every day."*
> —Frances Hesselbein

In his book *The New Leadership Paradigm*, internationally recognized author Richard Barrett talks about the importance of alignment to company values, commitment to the organization's vision, and personal accountability among employees. Without these three factors, he says, a company can experience high levels of *cultural entropy*, which he defines as "the degree of dysfunction in a human system caused by behaviours that are rooted in self-interest... [including] internal competition, blame, silo mentality, bureaucracy, empire-building, and so forth." And, he goes on to say, these types of behaviours generally start at the top.

As Barrett says, the culture of an organization is shaped by its senior leaders. Each and every person in an organization plays a significant role in executing its mission. Too often, individuals get lost in collective labels – associates, staff, workforce, employees, unions. Yet each person in an organization is an asset that is unique and worthy of respect. Each is personally accountable for contributing to the organization's success. Senior leaders can't mandate accountability, but they can create a culture that fosters engagement, commitment, and high performance.

The Ingredients of Culture

Organizational culture is connected to the concepts in this book. Perception, relationships, and behaviours each play a role in the health and well-being of an organization.

Culture is about *perceptions*. Culture is a description of *the way things get done* in an organization. It's also an organization's value proposition. It's about how people experience an organization and the degree to which they are pleased about where they work. As Peter

Part Two: Organizational Leadership Competencies

Drucker, noted management consultant and author, once said, "culture eats strategy for breakfast. It's not that strategy is unimportant – it's that culture is more powerful and empowering – a more successful route to organizational success."

Culture is about *relationships*. I had a client in the hospitality industry that had a mantra, "If you are not directly serving the customer, you better be serving the heck out of the people who are." Senior leaders need to think about how to create a culture that not only serves their customers, but their employees as well. You don't get loyal customers without loyal and committed workers. And you don't get loyal and committed workers without a leadership team that focuses on healthy relationships between the team leaders and those who deliver the services. How employees are treated translates into how customers are treated. To the extent that senior leaders treat their employees as valuable, important, and critical to their mission, the employees, in turn, treat their customers the same way.

When you consider the varied relationships in your organization, reflect on the fact that the most important relationships are those between your employees and their team leaders. When those relationships aren't productive, the predictable result is an unhealthy work environment. These environments are toxic. They are exemplified by low energy, poor morale, and decreased performance. When you transform to a productive culture, you improve the health of your organization and your performance too.

Culture is about *behaviours*. Culture is about how people behave. It's their common practices – how they interact with each other. An organization exhibits a healthy culture when people work together productively. There is energy and a high degree of discretionary effort. People are aligned with regard to how they live the values of the organization, and they do what needs to be done to survive and thrive. Virtually every successful business in history has developed a distinctive culture that is clearly identifiable by its employees. Most experts would agree that corporate culture is an important variable when it comes to a person's perception of an *employer of choice*.

COMPETENCY #12: Transform Culture

Pay Attention to the Symptoms of an Unhealthy Culture

We have talked about symptoms as *early warning signs*. As with health in general, when we notice symptoms, we tend to initially ignore them, hoping they will go away, but often they don't. They require some sort of treatment to get rid of the source of the problem. When it comes to organizational culture, it's wise to recognize the early warning signs that, when left unresolved, can escalate to more serious, high-cost issues that threaten the longer-term health of the organization. Remember, prevention is less expensive than the cure.

SYMPTOMS	⇒	HIGH-COST ISSUES
Increased absenteeism		Active resistance
Poor morale		High turnover
Health/stress leaves		Legal actions
Reduced performance		Open confrontations
Declining productivity		Severance/dismissals
Low-quality relationships		Formal discipline

Every symptom has a root cause. Politics, egos, territorial behaviours, misunderstandings, misperceptions, competitiveness – these are some of the most common root causes of an unhealthy culture. Some organizations build a culture of fear – fear of management or, ultimately, fear of losing one's job. In these cultures, each person's energy is put toward the game of CYA. It becomes a *blame someone else* culture. This type of culture poses a threat to every source of potential energy that's waiting to be tapped. If your culture is one of fear and insecurity, know that you are generating apathy and compliance. If your culture is one where there is little recognition for efforts and people are treated as commodities, you are generating anger and frustration.

Think of organizational cultures on a spectrum from *fear-driven* to *trust-driven*. A fear-driven culture is characterized by autocratic decision-making, with controlling rules and policies. The senior leadership is perceived to be saying, "Do what we tell you to do," and the employees, in return, think, "Management doesn't trust us." When people are continually told what to do, an organization becomes one of compliance and learned helplessness. People avoid taking risks because they fear

Part Two: Organizational Leadership Competencies

being seen as a failure. They do what they're told, they always agree with the boss, they play the politics, and they count the days to retirement.

While relationships are the foundation of effective leadership, a fear-based culture literally shakes that foundation. There is a definite cooling effect on relationships when people don't trust that their leaders have their best interests at heart.

Think about the current cultural practices of your organization, answering the following questions. Ask your colleagues on the executive team to answer these questions too. Look for similarities and differences in their responses. Explore those differences in perception.

- How do people relate to one another? How do they relate to your clients, customers, suppliers, and business partners?

- How do people make decisions? What do they pay attention to? How do people prioritize things?

- How do most employees view your organization? If you spoke with the people who chose to leave your organization, what might they share?

- How might new hires view your organization, seeing it through fresh eyes?

- What basic assumptions drive the behaviours across your organization?

- How are the organization's values demonstrated in the behaviours of your executive team and your team leaders?

What is Culture Transformation?

Michael Hammer and James Champy, authors of *Reengineering the Corporation*, write that many reengineering initiatives fail because they underestimate the human factor. The programs are well-designed with clear objectives, but if people aren't open to change, involved in it, and committed, the organization doesn't reap the intended benefits. Often, when that happens, new programs are introduced with the hope that they'll take hold. This never-ending cycle only breaks when leaders understand that culture reigns supreme. It's not the quality of the program; it's the culture that needs to be addressed. People can be the major obstacle to change. Sometimes the culture needs to change in order to improve employee engagement, boost productivity, and achieve higher levels of performance.

Culture transformation is about moving forward with the same change model we've looked at before – transitioning from a current state to a desired future state. The desired future is defined as the right culture for the organization. It is hard to imagine a future state that doesn't include productive relationships, aligned and cohesive teams, and engaged and committed people. So, if your current culture is missing these important variables, culture transformation could very well be what you need. It requires the commitment to transform to a future where each employee feels like they belong and wants to invest in the long-term success of your organization.

Is it Really Necessary?

There's an old saying that *happy employees are productive employees*. In reply to that statement, I once heard an executive vice-president say that the word *happy* didn't belong in business. He believed that it was not his job to ensure that employees were happy.

Perhaps the word happy didn't resonate. It's important to remember that people interpret words differently. What if we used a different word? To better influence this executive, we might have used the word *committed* or *engaged*. But regardless of the word used, this executive still had to come to grips with the same important point: When a person's work makes them feel worthwhile, their productivity reflects it. And the bottom line does, too.

Do You Have a Culture of Trust?

A culture of trust is one in which management trusts their employees to do the job they were hired to do and supports them in getting it done. In return, employees are energized and committed to their organization. This is a culture where you trust your employees, and they believe that you do; your employees trust you, and you believe that they do.

In a culture of trust, each person assumes the positive intent of every other person. There is a firm belief in the honesty, integrity, and reliability of each other person. Trust doesn't mean being naïve or gullible.

Part Two: Organizational Leadership Competencies

It means being open and empathetic – listening to learn and avoiding assumptions of intent. When there is a high degree of trust on and between teams, conflicts are prevented, where possible, and resolved quickly when they occur. It takes honest talk and congruent actions to create a culture of trust. The team leaders in your organization must ask more questions, listen more than they speak, and support truthful dialogue. Your job is to ensure that they do.

In a culture of trust, people are willing to take risks because they know they won't be punished for making well-intentioned mistakes. People are also more willing to speak their minds because they know what they say isn't going to be held against them. People become courageous because they perceive that they are not alone. In this type of culture, leaders ask: "What do you need?" and "How can I help?" They say, "Let's learn from our mistakes" and "Let's come up with solutions."

The Impact of Perception on Trust

Trust is directly connected to personal perspectives. As you now know, everyone comes to work with their own unique way of looking at things. They have their own expectations and interpretation of their organization – leadership, colleagues, and customers. Everything each person perceives is linked to their driver and their beliefs regarding "what it's like to work here." Their perspective is either it's a good place or a not-so-good place. This perception, of course, has nothing to do with reality. People believe what they see from their own perspective.

In a culture of trust, relationships are critical. The first thing you see is people willing to engage in open and honest dialogue. People are visibly supportive. People are accepted for who they are regardless of their intrinsic driver and their strengths. Everyone feels like they are in the loop when it comes to what's happening in the organization. Senior leaders wander around and stop to talk to employees at all levels of the organization – the top floor to the shop floor. People are encouraged to ask questions, and they expect to get answers. They feel safe to challenge those answers respectfully. Most importantly, there is visible energy. The work creates energy; it doesn't drain it. Work becomes the place where people *want to* contribute, rather than have to contribute. People reciprocate this sense of trust with hard work and the highest level of commitment.

Commitment is one of the most important factors for building a healthy culture. Commitment comes when leaders break through their mask of positional power, open up the dialogue, and behave in more trusting ways. When your leaders trust that the employees have good intentions, and your employees, in turn, trust that their leaders have good intentions, your organization has transformed into a culture of trust.

Commitment energizers are inherent in productive relationships; they include fairness, collaboration, open and honest dialogue, recognition, inclusion, and mutual trust between leaders and employees. Commitment impediments, on the other hand, come from non-productive relationships: mistrust between leaders and employees, lack of accountability, lack of motivation, and non-supportive management. Which would you prefer?

The Scale of Commitment

Each person consciously or unconsciously chooses a level of work commitment along this continuum.

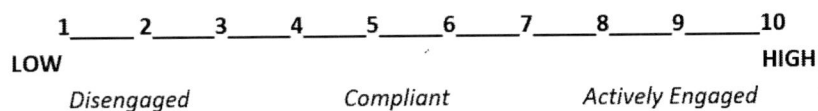

Someone who chooses level three or less is disengaged – it might be a good time for them to exit your organization. Someone who chooses levels four to seven is compliant – this person may be giving just enough discretionary effort to keep their job but is performing below their potential. They most definitely need an energy boost from their leaders. Someone who chooses levels eight to ten is actively engaged. They exhibit high energy and discretionary effort. They are passionate about their work. This level of commitment comes from a want to, or pull motivation, not a have to, or push motivation. Their engagement speaks to the heart of their sense of purpose; they are pulled toward work they see as meaningful. It provides insight into the answers to their questions: "Who am I? Why am I here? How can I contribute?"

Culture transformation must address how to get everyone in your organization to levels eight to ten. Remember the insights from Maslow's Hierarchy of Needs. There's a difference between growth needs and deficit needs. Our need for money and security are important when they're missing. However, once our financial and security needs are met, we need growth. We can get that growth either at work or elsewhere. If it comes from elsewhere, we're only staying in our jobs to pay the bills. Our work is not going to fulfill our needs for self-actualization and self-worth. It's hard to be passionate when you're just doing what you have to do.

In these situations, providing opportunities to learn and grow is key. When you think back to your own experiences, you may recall a leader who inspired and challenged you – someone from whom you wanted to learn. Encourage your team leaders to be that kind of person for their associates.

Your organization probably has many people between levels four and seven. Have they ever been inspired to do more? When people are willing to take risks or make mistakes, going beyond what is expected, are they rewarded for that behaviour, or are their actions punished or ignored? If your organization doesn't see the potential in allowing your people to make mistakes, learn, and grow, some of your most valuable people will eventually leave to contribute elsewhere.

The best way to find out what people need is to have your team leaders ask them! What do they need to be inspired and committed in their work? Now think about leadership actions that build commitment over compliance. Your actions may need to focus more on influence and less on control; more on asking, less on telling.

Time for Reflection

Organizations succeed or fail based on whether or not their people are willing to go the extra mile. Cultures that inspire and energize reap the benefits of a committed workforce. That's quite different from what happens in companies that manage people to ensure they show up on time, follow company policy, do what they're told, and put in a good day's work.

Imagine an organization that has been named an *employer of choice*. What might that organization do better than yours? Does it have a more committed and loyal workforce? Do its leaders inspire and grow their people to be more resilient and innovative? Has it reinvented its relationships with its employees? Cultural transformation starts by identifying the leadership practices that reinforce a culture of trust.

COMPETENCY #12: Transform Culture

What's the Formula?

Now that you have reflected on the importance of culture transformation, have your team look at your current culture and decide whether it's the one you want. Do you want to develop a culture of trust, purpose, commitment, and energy? Do you want highly engaged and committed people across your organization that contribute the highest performance potential rather than simply doing their job – where maximum energy goes toward creativity and problem-solving? What will you need to do to become that organization? What are your obstacles? What conditions need to exist before your organization can become a more fulfilling work environment?

To create the right culture, provide a compelling vision of what is possible and a mission that ignites the passion of your workplace. Then, trust your people to do the right things. *That's the formula for a healthy, integrated, high-performing organization.*

Determine whether your organization needs to shift to a culture that attracts and retains the best. Here are some questions for each member of your team to answer and reflect upon:

- What is our estimate of the commitment level of our organization on a scale of one to ten?

- What are the drivers of commitment in our organization?

- Why do we think good people leave our organization?

- Why are some people loyal?

- What is our level of commitment to keeping our best?

- What would change if the majority of our employees were more committed than they are now?

Imagine how people would work if your organization was working at peak performance. You never hear "it's not my job" in a culture of trust. Identify your employees' current behaviours and compare them to the desired behaviours. Create a vision of the kind of culture you want.

Part Two: Organizational Leadership Competencies

Finally, consider the most important components of a successful transformation:

1. **A clear and compelling purpose:** What we are doing and why it's worth doing. Do people see the link to desirable benefits? Do they perceive it as important from their perspective?

2. **Clear and impactful communication**: Can everyone visualize the change in practice? Are perceptions consistent with different perspectives?

3. **Consistent rewards and recognition**: Do the rewards and reasons for recognition support the required changes in behaviours?

Learning Nuggets

This competency is made up of the skills required to create a culture of trust, purpose, commitment, and energy.

Remember...

- ✓ Your culture reflects the norms, values, and beliefs that direct how things get done.
- ✓ Transformation means shifting toward a culture of productive relationships, trust, and commitment.
- ✓ Energy and commitment require the belief that a change is worthwhile and makes sense.
- ✓ To generate commitment, try to focus on influence, not control.
- ✓ Commitment emerges when people see opportunities, not obstacles.
- ✓ Address the visible symptoms of an unhealthy culture before harmful issues surface.

Now that you have reviewed the twelve leadership competencies, think about what is truly fundamental to the success of your organization in the face of a complex and competitive future. Reflect on the

COMPETENCY #12: TRANSFORM CULTURE

potential of your organization and how to unleash the energy that is often dormant. The commitment and loyalty of every individual is critical to the success of your organization. Your role is to grow that commitment and generate maximum energy. The future of your organization depends on you.

NEXT STEPS: PRACTICE

"One learns from books and example only that certain things can be done. Actual learning requires that you do those things."
—Frank Herbert

Moving from the *What* and the *Why* to the *How*

We only retain what we apply in practice. Consider how you can apply the Relationship Acuity insights you have acquired through this book to transform into the leader you aspire to be. The best way to do this is by practicing new behaviours and acquiring new skills.

No matter how much you expect it, doing the same things over and over won't get you a different result. If something has to change, you will need to reflect on what that change should be and why. A growing body of research confirms that when you reflect on your previous experience, it boosts your learning. This needs to be a continuous process. Get into the habit of asking yourself questions like, "Why did things turn out differently than I expected?" and "What have I learned from this experience?"

You Are Entering Part Three of Your Learning Journey

Learning represents a continuous cycle of **insight**, followed by **reflection** and moving through to **practice.**

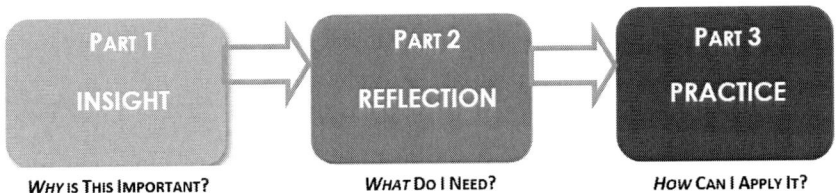

Insight Leads to Reflection

Part One of this book provided you with insights into *why* Relationship Acuity is important for your leadership development. These insights included understanding why your intrinsic driver, your perceptions, and your behaviours play such an important role in your development as a leader. These insights opened the door to understanding the twelve competencies that, together, create the building blocks for developing and sustaining productive work relationships. Embedded within each competency are specific skills and behaviours that you can practice and hone.

Reflection Leads to Understanding

Part Two included the opportunity to reflect on *what* the twelve critical leadership competencies involve. Think about the meaning of your insights in terms of the quality of your relationships. What's important about those insights? Consider their impact on the outcomes of your relationships. Remember some specific experiences you've had. What have been your most critical challenges when working with others? Then ask yourself what's working and what's not working in your relationships. Clarify what needs to change. Link the change to what's important to you. Ask yourself: "What's in it for me to change? Do I have a vested interest in doing things differently?" How might I approach a similar situation in the future? How will I put these insights into action?"

Practice Leads to Change

Now you likely recognize the importance of applying these insights in your current role. The *Relationship Acuity Leadership Guidebook* represents **Part Three** of your learning. This *Guidebook* leads you through the *how*. It includes practical strategies and actions designed to help you keep your work relationships healthy and productive. While insight and reflection are critical to new learning, your goal needs to be one that applies this learning. We all know how hard it is to get out of our comfort zones. We naturally want to resort back to doing what feels right and normal. However, if you really want to build productive relationships, it can only happen through sustained effort and practice. Continue to apply new and different ways of relating to others by being mindful of each unique person and situation you encounter. Over time, you will no doubt experience better outcomes.

For further information on how to acquire a copy of the *Guidebook*, email **info@ralsolutions.ca** or visit **www.relationshipacuity.ca**.

Next Steps: Practice

Start with Your Own Personal Gap Analysis

Refer to the gap analysis first introduced in Competency #7. Now, focus on the leadership competencies *you* want to build. Consider your current state, your desired future state, and the gap between the two. This is your application framework for building and sustaining Relationship Acuity.

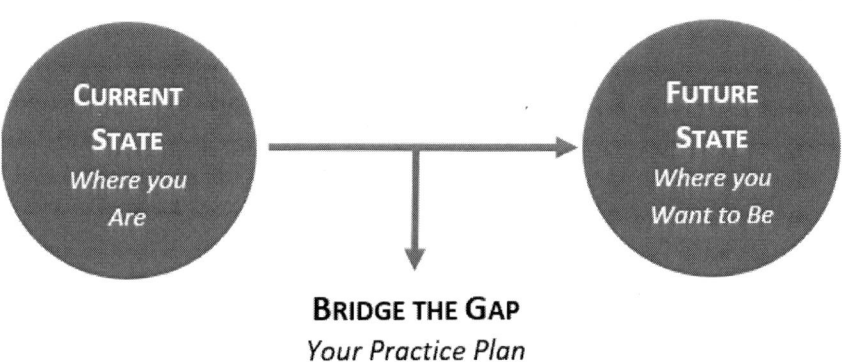

Start by reflecting on your current state – where you are now. You might think about people who constantly frustrate you. You may recall situations that didn't work out as you expected. You may need to improve your approach. Perhaps you're experiencing a specific personal or interpersonal conflict. Maybe there's an important issue that you've been unable to resolve. Whatever is happening, try to identify the root cause of each dilemma you're experiencing. That's what needs to change.

Once you have identified what needs to change and why, you are ready to picture your future state – where you want to be. Visualize what's happening in this new state: Things you have started doing (new behaviours you have strengthened), things you have stopped doing (misapplied behaviours you have reduced or eliminated), and/or things you have continued doing (productive behaviours that you continue to practice and reinforce).

Now, you are now ready to bridge the gap. Use the Relationship Acuity Leadership Guidebook to help you create a practice plan that takes you to where you need to be.

Your learning journey continues…

A FEW FINAL WORDS

Writing this book has been my own personal learning journey. I spent months reflecting on my professional experiences throughout my career, discovering what I believed were the most important insights to share. And I gained more insights along the way.

It is odd that I am completing this book at a time of unprecedented change in our world. It is apparent that some businesses won't survive, while others will grow and thrive. New ways of working are being developed every day.

At the same time, we are in the midst of critical relationship issues between countries, between government leaders, and between ordinary citizens and the people who are hired to serve them. People are risking their health to attend demonstrations with thousands of people who share a sense of purpose that takes precedence over fear. It is a powerful indicator of the energy that comes from this power of purpose.

They say it takes a crisis for change, and this crisis is the most influential change current generations have experienced. It presents new challenges. What will the new world of work look like? What will be the impact on work relationships when individuals and teams meet virtually more frequently than face-to-face? How will people connect personally? How will they learn from each other? If people feel isolated, what will be the impact on their work productivity? Only time will tell.

Remember that each person's internal driver comes from their sense of purpose that is rooted in their need for self-worth. Motivation is a powerful force. It influences how people look at the world. Perceptions differ, and they are often visible in our actions and words. Be mindful of their impact. Consider how others might perceive you and what assumptions they might make about why you do what you do. And don't forget that you can choose your response in different situations, with people who don't see the world the way you do. With the leadership challenges ahead, these insights will serve you well. You are now looking at leadership through a different lens.

INSPIRING PSYCHOLOGISTS, AUTHORS, AND EDUCATORS

Relationship Acuity: Leadership Through a Different Lens can be read as a comprehensive survey course on some of the most important concepts in leadership. It was inspired by a long list of psychologists, authors, educators, and researchers – particularly those listed here (most of whom are also cited throughout the book). For a deeper look into perception, motivation, and relationships, and the twelve leadership competencies I've discussed, please refer to the work of these inspiring people.

Karl Albrecht
Richard Barrett
Dr. Warren Bennis
Dr. Ken Blanchard
Dr. William Bridges
Dr. John O. Burdett
Dr. Robert Cialdini
James S. Coleman
Dr. Stephen R. Covey
Dr. Edward L. Deci
Dr. Albert Ellis
Dr. Tasha Eurich
Dr. Viktor Frankl
Daniel Goleman
Dr. Heidi Grant-Halvorson
Sheila Heen
Dr. Ronald Heifetz
Dr. Frederick Herzberg
Dr. Karen Horney
Dr. Dennis T. Jaffe
Dr. Daniel Kahneman
Robert B. Kaiser
Dr. Robert E. Kaplan
Dr. Beverly Kaye

Deborah Khoshaba
Dr. John Kotter
Dr. James M. Kouzes
Dr. Robert J. Kriegel
Dr. Elisabeth Kübler-Ross
Patrick Lencioni
Marty Linsky
Dr. Salvatore Maddi
Dr. Robert F. Mager
Dr. Abraham Maslow
Dr. David McClelland
David McNally
Art McNeil
Darren Overfield
Dr. Bruce Patton
Dr. Elias H. Porter
Dr. Barry Z. Posner
Dr. Marshall Sashkin
Dr. Cynthia D. Scott
Simon Sinek
Dr. Douglas Stone
Dr. Bruce Tuckman
Dr. Margaret Wheatley
Dr. Amy Wrzesniewski

BIBLIOGRAPHY

INTRODUCTION

Bennis, Warren. *Why Leaders Can't Lead: The Unconscious Conspiracy Continues.* San Francisco: Jossey Bass, 1989.

RELATIONSHIPS MATTER

Kouzes, James M. and Posner, Barry Z. *How to Get Extraordinary Things Done in Organizations.* San Francisco: Jossey-Bass, 1987.

Mann, Charles Riborg. Extrapolated from *A Study of Engineering Education.* Carnegie Foundation, 1918. Pages 106-107.

THE WHY FACTOR

Hurst, Aaron. *The Purpose Economy, How Your Desire for Impact, Personal Growth and Community is Changing the World.* Boise: Elevate, 2014.

Maslow, Abraham H. *A Theory of Human Motivation.* Psychological Review, *1943, 50*(4), 370–396

Kriegel, Robert J. and Patler, Louis. *If It Ain't Broke... BREAK IT! And Other Unconventional Wisdom for a Changing Business World.* New York: Warner Books Inc., 1991, page 13.

Deci, E. L. & Ryan, R. M. *Self-determination Theory: A Macrotheory of Human Motivation, Development, and Health.* Canadian Psychology: Canadian Psychological Association 2008, Vol. 49, No. 3, pp 182–185.

McClelland, David. *Human Motivation.* Cambridge University Press, 1987.

Horney, Karen. *The Neurotic Personality of our Time.* W. W. Norton & Company; Revised edition, 1994.

Porter, Elias. *On the Development of Relationship Awareness™ Theory.* Personal Strengths Publishing, Inc. 1976.

Relationship Acuity: Leadership Through a *Different* Lens

THE PERCEPTION CONNECTION

Kahneman, Daniel. *Thinking Fast and Slow.* New York: Farrar, Strauss and Giroux, 2011.

Wason, Peter C. *On the Failure To Eliminate Hypotheses In A Conceptual Task.* The Quarterly Journal of Experimental Psychology, *12,* 1960, pp 129–140.

RELATIONSHIP ACUITY COMPETENCIES

McClelland, David C. *Testing for Competence Rather Than for "Intelligence."* American Psychologist, January 1973.

Kotter, John P. *The Leadership Factor.* New York Free Press, 1988.

George, Bill. *True North: Becoming an Authentic Leader.* San Francisco: Jossey-Bass, 2007.

COMPETENCY #1

McNally, David. *Even Eagles Need a Push: Learning to Soar in a Changing World.* New York: Dell Publishing, 1990.

Scott, Sarah. *Do Grades Really Matter?* Maclean's Magazine, Sept. 10, 2007.

Kaye, Beverly & Winkle Giulioni, Julie. *Help Them Grow or Watch Them Go: Career Conversations Employees Want.* San Francisco: Berrett-Koehler Publishers, Inc. 2012.

COMPETENCY #2

Kaiser, Robert B. and Overfield, Darren V. *Strengths, Strengths Overused, And Lopsided Leadership.* Consulting Psychology Journal: Practice and Research, American Psychological Association 2011, Vol. 63, No. 2, pp 89–109.

Kaplan, Bob with Kaiser, Bob. *The Versatile Leader: Make the Most of Your Strengths Without Overdoing It.* San Francisco: John Wiley & Sons, Inc. 2006.

Bibliography

COMPETENCY #3

Cialdini, Robert B. *Influence: The Psychology of Persuasion.* New York: William Morrow and Co. Inc., 1993.

Useem, Michael. *Leading Up: The Art of Managing Your Boss.* Knowledge@Wharton, Wharton University of Pennsylvania, April 25, 2001.

COMPETENCY #4

Goleman, Daniel. *Emotional Intelligence: Why it Can Matter More than IQ.* New York: Bantam Dell, 1995.

Sashkin, Marshall. *Conflict Style Inventory.* HRD Press, 1990.

COMPETENCY #5

Maddi, Salvatore R. *Hardiness: Turning Stressful Circumstances into Resilient Growth.* New York: Springer Dordrecht Heidelberg, 2013.

Ellis, Albert. *Rational Psychotherapy and Individual Psychology.* Journal of Individual Psychology 13: pp 38-44.

Maddi, Salvatore R. and Khoshaba, Deborah M. *How to Succeed No Matter What Life Throws at You.* New York: AMACOM – American Management Association, 2005.

Scott, Cynthia and Jaffe, Dennis. *Survive and Thrive in Times of Change.* Training and Development Journal, April 1988.

COMPETENCY #8

Kislik, Liz. *How to Get the Best From Each Team Member.* Forbes, September 3, 2020.

Coleman, James A. *Foundations of Social Theory.* Cambridge, Mass: Harvard University Press, 1990.

Tuckman, Bruce W. *Tuckman, Developmental Sequence in Small Groups.* Psychological Bulletin, 1965, 63(6).

Relationship Acuity: Leadership Through a *Different* Lens

COMPETENCY #9

Heifetz, Ronald and Linsky, Marty. *Leadership on the Line: Staying Alive Through the Dangers of Leading.* Harvard Business Review Press; Revised edition, July 2017.

Stone, Douglas et al. *Difficult Conversations: How to Discuss What Matters Most.* New York: The Penguin Group, 1999.

COMPETENCY #10

McKinsey & Company, *Changing Change Management.* Article, July 1, 2015.

Mohr, Bernard J. and Magruder Watkins, Jane. *The Essentials of Appreciative Inquiry: A Roadmap for Creating Positive Futures.* Pegasus Communications, June 2002.

Bridges, William. *Managing Transitions: Making the Most of Change.* Addison-Wesley Publishing Company, Reading Massachusetts, 1991.

ORGANIZATIONAL LEADERS GENERATE CORPORATE ENERGY

McNeil, Art. *The "I" of the Hurricane: Creating Corporate Energy.* Toronto: Stoddart Publishing Co. Limited, 1987.

Groysberg, Boris et al. *The Culture Factor.* Harvard Business Review, January–February 2018 issue.

COMPETENCY #11

Lencioni, Patrick. *Make Your Values Mean Something.* Harvard Business Review Article, July 2002.

COMPETENCY #12

Barrett, Richard. *The New Leadership Paradigm: Leading Self, Leading Others, Leading an Organization, Leading in Society.* New York: Lulu.com, 2011.

Hammer, Michael and Champy, James. *Reengineering the Corporation: A Manifesto for Business Revolution.* London: GB, Nicholas Brealey Publishing Limited, 1993.

ABOUT THE AUTHOR

Judy Hemmingsen is a founding Partner of RA Leadership Solutions Inc. She is the author of Relationship Acuity: Leadership Through a *Different* Lens and co-author of the Relationship Acuity Leadership *Guide*book. She has a passion for helping leaders develop the strategies they need to achieve optimum performance in their organizations. Through RA Leadership Solutions Inc., her primary focus is to help leaders understand the importance of Relationship Acuity®, a unique approach for people, at all levels of an organization, to collaborate productively in today's complex and diverse work environments.

Judy has acquired extensive experience in industry, government, and consulting organizations, with a focus on leadership coaching and facilitated learning. Her corporate business experience includes senior HR and OD positions in the areas of recruitment, talent development and organization effectiveness. As a Senior Consultant with a major human capital management firm, she coached executives and developed numerous workshops and presentations for leaders and teams in a large variety of industries and sectors. Most recently, she spent 11 years as the Managing Partner in the Canadian operation of a global business, consulting and training with a suite of relationship building tools.

Judy has a Master's in Clinical Psychology, specializing in Assessment and Psychotherapeutic Counselling, and Certificates in Alternative Dispute Resolution (ADR) and Mediation. She is a member of the Canadian Institute for Learning and Development (I4PL).

She can be reached at www.relationshipacuity.ca